A JOURNEY INTO GOD

DELIA SMITH

A Journey into God

Hodder & Stoughton
LONDON SYDNEY AUCKLAND TORONTO

The scripture quotations are taken from *The Jerusalem Bible* (©
Darton, Longman and Todd Ltd and Doubleday and Company Inc,
1966, 1967 and 1968), sometimes with the author's own rendering
and from *The Psalms: a new translation* (© The Grail 1963).
The lyrics from *Pattern* on page 15 are © Paul Simon and
reproduced by kind permission of Pattern Music.

British Library Cataloguing in Publication Data

Smith, Delia
    A journey into God.
    1. Christian life. Prayer
    I. Title
    248.3'2

    ISBN 0-340-49044-6

Published by Hodder and Stoughton,
a division of Hodder and Stoughton Ltd,
Mill Road, Dunton Green, Sevenoaks, Kent TN13 2YE
Editorial Office: 47 Bedford Square, London WC1B 3DP.

Photoset by Rowland Phototypesetting Ltd,
Bury St Edmunds, Suffolk

Printed in Great Britain by
St Edmundsbury Press Ltd, Bury St Edmunds, Suffolk

For Michael,
with love

CONTENTS

PREFACE

Prayer is something that God does. If only we could grasp this simple truth. The trouble is that this something that God does is essentially mystery: there are no neat formulas, no amount of books on prayer can ever reveal just what it is that God does.

First and foremost prayer is a relationship in which God is the initiator, constantly seeking to elicit a human response. It is an ongoing relationship, and like any other it can't be programmed or labelled and packaged – 'this is prayer, fullstop!' Prayer is life: living, growing, developing, but always in secret – like a tiny seed buried in the earth steadily yet imperceptibly thrusting itself upward to the light.

What is it that impels this seed upward? We know the earth and the rain sustain its growth, but what awakens it to life? That is mystery, something that God does. Prayer is precisely like that: something mysterious within that gently pushes *us* towards that albeit unidentified light, which will ultimately bring us to the blossoming of our full potential and answer all our deepest longings.

This book does not attempt to unravel the mystery, nor offer any techniques or formulas. But hopefully it will encourage others to yield themselves to this deepest and hidden aspect of human growth and life.

Anne Elliot, the heroine of Jane Austen's *Persuasion*, admits she is quite eloquent when giving advice to others on a subject that in her own life 'could ill bear examination'. I can identify completely with her, and am anxious to point out that what is contained in these pages is offered by one who shares the struggle, who is still journeying and not one who has in any sense arrived anywhere.

The journey into God is one in which the whole human

family is involved and (I believe) the response of each individual is inextricably bound up with everyone else's as a shared experience. What I, most of all, want to share with others is my own great hope in God, that he is indeed Lord, creator and lover of all that is, and that however murky our journey we will all eventually arrive at the point where we finally and fully recognise this truth: 'God saw all he had made and indeed it was very good.' As a human race we may not yet fully believe in God, but from the beginning God has always totally believed in us. That is my conviction, echoing the English mystic Julian of Norwich, who perceived that ultimately 'all shall be well'.

In order to encourage people to reflect more deeply and slowly, I have divided my thoughts into short sections which can be used on a daily basis, or from time to time whichever suits (it is also no accident that each chapter corresponds to a week). If a person is genuinely seeking God, God will undoubtedly meet them where they are and in whatever way they are best able to receive him. All I have set out to do here is provide a starting point, a springboard in which my own convictions and experiences are offered and shared.

Delia Smith
1988

ACKNOWLEDGMENTS

A big thank you to Michael, my husband, for his kind, long-suffering editing of my undisciplined scribble. Special thanks to Debbie Owen, Eric Major, Ruth Burrows, Wendy Beckett and Father Ron Rolheiser for their friendship, support and encouragement. And finally a thank you to Marie Neal, our secretary, and to Colly Colwell for the beautiful jacket design.

CHAPTER ONE

In the Beginning God . . .

TRUTH, WHAT IS THAT?

I yearn for truth but shall not reach it till I reach the source.

ROBERT BROWNING

Prayer in its simplest form is a one-word description of a whole lifetime's journey into God, a single word encompassing all that is central to human life. This is my conviction: that from the moment life begins prayer begins, like an underground spring, hidden and deep yet an undercurrent that pushes its way through the many layers of human complexity to a level where it can spill out into moments of consciousness.

Anyone who lives, prays. Anyone who possesses human life possesses a deeper spiritual life as well, and the journey of prayer is nothing more nor less than a gradual awakening to the reality of recognising what is already there.

In one of his poems Gerard Manley Hopkins describes this reality as 'a dearest freshness, deep down things'. He asserts that in all of life's 'trade and toil, smudge and smell' something fresh and beautiful exists within. In one way or another we can all recognise this spiritual undercurrent. Is there anyone who hasn't experienced these 'deep-down' moments in the normal course of life, moments in everyday life which somehow tap this underground spring – art, beauty, birth, achievement, sometimes even the most ordinary events in our daily existence that for a moment become transformed?

How difficult it is to put words to these experiences. The writers of antiquity, grappling with language, described it as a response, a spontaneous moment of pure love when encountering something of beauty. Later on – from the perspective of a more specific belief – it is simply an implicit response of love: in loving what is created we are directly or indirectly loving the creator. I recall my grandmother, who had no particular religious belief herself, gazing reflectively one day at a lilac tree in full bloom highlighted by the sun. 'If they looked at that,' she said, 'how could anyone say there isn't a God?' Such is the moment when prayer is the deep undercurrent breaking through: the impulse to search for, and identify, the creator in a more explicit way is how conscious prayer begins to happen.

Somewhere in the deeper regions of our existence there is a yearning for beauty and love, for purpose and meaning. We can, and do, keep this yearning at bay because one of our many paradoxes can be an inscrutable pessimism. We dare not believe that these things are really within our reach. Because this yearning tends to surface during the quieter and more reflective moments of life, we can stifle it by sheer activity and by being caught on the treadmill of living.

Yet for all this, those deep-down things can inexorably break through and confront us. We have a vivid example in history of this happening to a man – Pontius Pilate, who was anxious to wash his hands of the bother of those unruly Jews. Caught between the savage demands of the rabble and the intuitive pleas of his own wife, he was forced to interrogate his mysterious prisoner. '*Are* you a king?' 'Yes . . . and those who are on the side of truth listen to what I say.' Suddenly the ultimate question disarms this man of authority. 'Truth? What is that?' (John 18: 38) For a moment his security is threatened; he is pulled in two directions.

Who has not, at some time or another, had to grapple with this question? Oral tradition says that Pilate subsequently began a search for the answer and became a convert. But whether he did or not, his dilemma is common to all of us. Do we stifle this disturbing question, or do we seek to find answers and concede to that undercurrent of inner yearning which launches us on a journey of prayer?

In the Beginning God . . .

*I stepped down into the most hidden depth of my
being, lamp in hand and ears alert, to discover
whether in the deepest recesses of the blackness
within me I might not see the glint of the waters of
the current that flows on, whether I might not hear
the murmur of the mysterious waters that rise from
the uttermost depths, and will burst forth no man
knows where. With terror and intoxicating emotion, I realised that my poor trifling existence was
one with the immensity of all that is and all that is in
the process of becoming.*

TEILHARD DE CHARDIN

SETTING OUT

It was by faith that Abraham obeyed the call to set out for the country that was the inheritance given to him and his descendants, and that he set out without knowing where he was going. By faith he arrived, as a foreigner, in the Promised Land, and lived there as if in a strange country.

HEBREWS 11: 8–9

Although the sonorous Victorian language of some of our great hymns is not the vogue nowadays, there are some significant truths expressed in them. I have never much cared for John Henry Newman's 'Lead kindly light', finding the encircling gloom a somewhat morbid concept. However there is one line in it which I do feel makes a profound statement about prayer: 'I do not ask to see the distant scene, *one* step enough for me.' We might express it today as taking each day as it comes, or perhaps a younger person might call it 'just playing it by ear'.

What I want to say at the outset is that faith is definitely not a leap in the dark, and should never be described as such for that trivialises it into little more than a fantasy. Faith is not a blind venture, nor should we think of it as entailing a sacrifice of understanding. On the contrary, faith sets out with a hidden kind of pre-understanding – in the hope that more specific understanding will be given. True faith always questions, always searches out and – most importantly of all – always desires. It is here that prayer begins, with faith that is essentially the conscious desire of a person for understanding of what and who God is.

[6]

The journey is one of searching, reflecting, and being receptive so that the inward reflection begins to penetrate outward. Authentic prayer is rooted in the ordinary experience of daily life, which begins gradually to take on a new freshness. It is hard to improve on the simplicity of the Bible, which describes the spiritual journey as a gradual awakening from sleep, or a healing of blind eyes and deaf ears: there occurs, at a deep level, more and more sight, more and more hearing, more and more understanding – and all this happens in our experience of daily life.

Yet there is an obstacle to this desire for understanding. It seems to me that we live in an age where people for the most part have lost touch with this sense of the spiritual. There was a time when God was for people a palpable reality, while the world was shrouded in mystery. Now the opposite has happened: in our tremendous surge of knowledge about the world and the universe God has somehow been eclipsed. It has indeed been an exciting era of human development, and our microscopes and telescopes and satellites in space would appear to have given us most answers to most questions. With the aid of computer technology we can chart our progression from the first big bang, through billions of years of 'random' molecular activity, to our culmination as a human race. In our age of scientific enlightenment the human race seems to have grown greater and God has grown smaller.

We have lost our sense of mystery or, at best, are uncomfortable when confronted with it. It is a tragic loss and I sense it has somehow diminished us as human beings. Take human relationships: why do love affairs grow cold, why does the chase so often prove more fascinating than the conquest? Surely because when we have full knowledge, when we can confidently package and label our experience it has become plain boring.

I recently heard a top fashion-buyer talking about her work, how difficult and dangerous it was to determine so far ahead something as volatile as fashion. Choose a colour that doesn't take off or the wrong hemline, and a whole season's profits are lost. But it was precisely, she admitted, this element of mystery that stimulated her!

God is wild, wrote an American priest. He cannot be tamed or tied down. God is, always will be, mystery, and faith is essentially taking a chance on mystery. Without seeing the distant scene, we set out. Like Abraham we don't know where we are going; we are invited to journey into a strange and unfamiliar country, to learn to understand, to claim our inheritance which is the gradual unfolding of that peace and harmony which is our safest and truest home.

> *It is not always necessary that truth should find a tangible embodiment. Enough if it hovers as a spiritual essence and induces harmony by its vibrations, like the bell toll of solemn serenity.*
>
> GOETHE

INSIDE AND OUTSIDE

*Being admonished to return to myself I entered into
my own depths, with you as guide, and I was able to
do it because you were my helper . . . For behold you
were within me and I outside, and I sought you
outside. You were with me and I was not with you.*

ST AUGUSTINE

In a recent BBC television series (called *The Seven Ages*)
Ronald Eyre was interviewing different age-groups, one of
which consisted of people in their mid-forties. Much of that
particular programme revolved around what is often called
'mid-life crisis', which several speakers seemed to equate with
a crisis of identity. Who am I? What is the purpose of my
existence? One lady, however, who had been through a severe
breakdown had come through the experience with great inner
strength. She was quite definite about what had been her
salvation: 'Me. I discovered that bit of myself that is *truly* me.'

True, no mention was made of any religious significance but I
do believe this represents one of the most authentic religious
experiences, because self-knowing is God-knowing. Through
her painful journey she had arrived at a deep peace: instead of
struggling to be this, that or the other she was now content just
to be. The external struggles and tensions of life cannot be
escaped of course, but there *is* an inner self – St Augustine's
'own depths' – that can grow stronger through experiences
such as the one described.

The two levels of existence may be distinguished as, on the one
level the mind, the body and the senses, and on the other level

[9]

the soul or the spiritual life. I think it is true to say that one doesn't need to have any specific religious belief to be conscious that there is a part of our human make-up that operates on a deeper, spiritual level. But, equally, it is a distortion to view the two as distinct and unrelated, as if the soul was something that enters a body during its earthly life, then takes leave of it afterwards and scoots off somewhere else. The two are inseparably bound together and, I believe, to God.

To illustrate this relationship, reflect for a moment on this story of a little boat. The boat has been finely built, strong and seaworthy, but it is not entirely complete. There are fitments missing and in its completion it will receive a beautiful coat of bright paint that will render it quite different from any other boat ever built. It has a set of oars and a sturdy sail, and there is a helmsman in charge of sailing it across the high seas to the harbour it needs to reach for its completion. The helmsman however is entirely free to do as he wishes: he can leave the boat incomplete, or he can take his chance against the waves and tide and try to find a more accessible harbour which can do bits of the work.

As it turns out he makes little headway with the oars, but he has an alternative – he can hoist the sail. Then he is at the mercy of the wind, and all he can do is watch and wait and respond to the wind. Sometimes it will be strong and he will move at a cracking speed: at other times he will have to content himself with the gentlest of breezes where no progress seems to be made at all. Maybe he will even get fed up and row back to wherever he came from. *But* if he's patient and responsive and surrenders himself to the wind, it will eventually lead him safely across the ocean to the harbour of completion.

The boat is me (or you). The oars represent our physical and mental powers, the helmsman our heart and will. The sail is the soul and the wind is, to use the biblical expression, the breath of God which animates the soul. We can work with the oars to complete life by our own powers, or we can hoist the sail, entering into a spiritual journey of prayer, and co-operate with the wind by accepting its mysterious invisible presence, and thus steer ourselves in the right direction for home.

> *After saying these things he looked about him, and he saw the pilot of his ship standing by the helm and gazing down now at the full sails and now at the distance.*
> *And he said, patient ever patient is the captain of my ship. The wind blows and restless are the sails; even the rudder begs direction. Now they shall wait no longer. I am ready.*
> *The stream has reached the sea and now the great mother holds her son against her breast.*

KAHLIL GIBRAN: *The Prophet*

ONLY HE WHO SEES

*Earth is crammed with heaven and every
common bush on fire with God.
But only he who sees takes off his shoes, the rest
sit and pluck blackberries.*

ELIZABETH BARRETT BROWNING

In this short verse Elizabeth Browning has, for me, captured the essence of what prayer is. The reference is of course to Moses' encounter with the burning bush, his moment of understanding who God was. Moses was a man of stature, a royal prince taught all the wisdom of the Egyptians, yet this experience, this discovery of his true self, took place, it will be recalled, after a long and lonely spell looking after sheep on the mountains. From the heart of the fire Moses' name is called: 'take off your shoes for the place on which you stand is holy ground' (Exodus 3: 6).

God is not to be found in human wisdom and learning, nor by people with special privileges of intuition and understanding, nor yet through self-contrived transcendentalism (as some modern cults prescribe). Perhaps what distinguishes the Jewish and Christian traditions from others is that they are firmly rooted in the earth – 'the earth is crammed with heaven' – and in the commonplace of daily life. The closer a person comes to God the more he is 'seen' in the normality of day-to-day existence.

Yet who is it that 'sees' God in the events of ordinary daily life? Are some people more sensitive, special in some way? And who are the blackberry pluckers? The key to these questions perhaps lies in the fact that Moses encountered God when he had deliberately taken time off to be alone.

There is a time when we all, figuratively speaking, need to wander off from the pressure of life and simply be alone. Prayer begins with space, no more and no less. Forget any magic formulas, and start with ordinary spaces and lonely places – like bus queues, train journeys, walks. If you want to get really earthy, the answer I once heard a priest give to a lady who protested she had no 'spaces' was how about a sinkful of dirty dishes. Now there's a lonely place!

People lose the experience of God when they lose the experience of space: things become too familiar when we no longer have the time to perceive the unfamiliar. We get caught up in the wrong kind of self-preoccupation where (as in a previous analogy) *we* do the rowing of the boat. But all this is an escape from our true selves, for we are afraid to encounter God, to stand on the holy ground. 'Mummy, mummy' cries the excited seven-year-old, who has still not lost that precious sense of wonder. 'Come and look at the sunset!'

'I'm busy making a cake,' comes the reply.

'But, Mummy, you can make a cake anytime. There'll never be a sunset like this one.'

All right, you may say, the sun rises and sets every single day, it's quite an ordinary event. But it is God who is in the ordinary and we who are outside it.

We can so easily settle for being blackberry pluckers, busy yet too lazy to really set out and 'see' the wonder of God, who doesn't exist in some faraway inaccessible dwelling nor needs to be sought in temples or shrines. No, he's so close. Right at the ends of our noses so to speak, in the whole of creation – but only he who sees takes off his shoes.

A Journey into God

The world is charged with the grandeur of God.
It will flame out, like shining from shook foil;
It gathers to a greatness, like the ooze of oil
Crushed. Why do men then not reck his rod?
Generations have trod, have trod, have trod;
And all is seared with trade; bleared, smeared with toil;
And wears man's smudge and shares man's smell: the soil
Is bare now, nor can foot feel, being shod.

GERARD MANLEY HOPKINS

WANTING GOD

*If we go down into ourselves, we find that we
possess exactly what we desire.*

SIMONE WEIL

We've all experienced the sentiments behind the expression
'my heart isn't really in it': on one level we can be engaged in
some occupation, yet on another we're not really involved at
all. It is probably too simple to say that we operate just on two
levels – life is a complexity of many layers – but it is at the very
deepest level that truth and reality exist, albeit unrecognised,
even unsought. Just as God is a mystery, so are we a mystery to
ourselves and can choose to live for the most part on the
superficial level, ignoring the reality within. As Paul Simon put
it in one of his earliest songs, describing twilight shadows
reflected on the wall of a room: 'impaled upon the wall my eyes
can dimly see the patterns of my life and the puzzle that is me'.

Out of the puzzle, though, one thing can emerge if we allow it
to and this is desire: what I *truly* wish and hope for, that is
what is most real. I can be crippled with shyness and yet dearly
want to be outgoing. I can be paralysed when it comes to
showing love and yet truly and deeply love nonetheless. A
person suffering from depression doesn't actually want to be
depressed. There are endless examples of doing (or being)
what we don't want, and not doing what we want.

It is only on this deep, spiritual level that God sees and hears us.
He understands what we really are and what we really want.
This is at the same time both reassuring and frightening,
because although it cuts right through all the crippling fears,
apprehension and lack of self-expression, it likewise makes

[15]

short work of the sham and hypocrisy that so often goes in the name of 'religion'.

The Pharisees in the Gospels were masters of spiritual sham, keeping up the outward show of religious fervour with no real desire for God; way ahead of the so-called religious of the day, it was the prostitutes and tax-collectors who were nearer to a relationship with God. And nothing has changed today. With prayer all that is still significant is whether a person really *wants* to know God or not. The only prerequisite is desire, however faint or unfelt, or as one lady asked on a retreat, 'Is it enough to want to want?' Yes, is the emphatic answer. Like the prostitutes and tax-collectors, whatever our struggles are, however muddy and murky is the road we travel, if we want to make the journey we will come to possess what we most desire. People who don't drive because they 'never had time to take a lesson', didn't actually want to drive at base. No one can afford to put time and effort into anything unless they really do want it.

What we shall see later on is that in fact all our desires, everything that we wish to possess or achieve, are a longing for God. All we pursue in search of fulfilment is this deepest desire in disguise. Augustine put it most eloquently: 'I sought you outside and fell upon those lovely things that you had made. I was kept from you by those things, yet had they not been in you they would not have been at all.' He said something else too: 'Desire never ceases to pray for ever; though the tongue is silent, if there is desire then there is prayer.'

> *More than all else, keep watch over your heart,*
> *since here are the wellsprings of life.*

PROVERBS 4: 23

THE MYTH OF
INDEPENDENCE

The highest reason for human dignity is man's vocation to communion with God. From the outset man is invited to a close familiarity with God. He only exists because God's love created and continually sustains him. Nor does he live fully and truly unless he freely acknowledges that love and commits himself to his Creator.

The Church in the Modern World

No man is an island sufficient unto himself, wrote the seventeenth-century poet John Donne, and I think he might have added that nor is the whole human race ever sufficient unto itself. In our quest for God it may be useful to consider what the opposite of God is; and that is self-sufficient man, autonomous and independent. The absence of God implies substituting man in his place – man knowing all and controlling all.

Essentially this is the moral point at the heart of the fabled story of Adam and Eve. At the beginning man and woman are part of a shared life, living *with* God: that means they are the recipients from God of life and everything needed to sustain it, which in turn involves a certain vulnerability on their part. But they also have freedom, the freedom to be persuaded that increasing their knowledge will put them on an equal footing with God, no longer dependent but independent.

Knowledge is power! It has been the rallying-cry of the independents throughout history. Independence of God did not stop with Adam and Eve: from Plato's philosophically ideal society to Hitler's obscene final solution mankind has continued to hanker after the vanity of self-sufficiency. Human nature being what it is, the urge to be in control of one's life does not stop there. Sooner or later it needs to control others' lives as well.

If we are resourceful, in positions of effective power, we can create the mirage of independence up to a point. But a mirage is all it is. As the psalmist says 'Great men are only an illusion; placed on the scales they rise, they weigh less than a breath' (61/62), and elsewhere: 'Life is over like a sigh; it springs up in the morning but by evening it withers and fades' (89/90). Great men cannot supply the answers to the problems of pain and suffering, nor death itself. The scandal of total extinction is beyond the powers of dictators' philosophies and social reforms to solve. When Marx described religion as the cry of the oppressed creature, he was speaking of poverty and inequality; but what is more oppressive than man's powerlessness in the face of death?

It seems to me that perhaps the human race has to experience the futility of independence before it can choose the other option. The prodigal son, if you recall, only found living in communion with his father desirable *after* he had worked through his desire for independence and discovered his own incomplete and limited resources. If man's vocation is communion with God, then independence in the end is utterly futile.

Communion with God involves shared existence and a loss of independence. It means that the answers I seek are beyond myself, and in order to receive them I must become vulnerable to something beyond my own resources, break out of my self-protective shell and learn how to trust the God who invites me to this close familiarity with himself.

> *Then his son said, 'Father, I have sinned against heaven and against you. I no longer deserve to be called your son.' But the father said to his servants,*

[18]

'Quick! Bring out the best robe and put it on him; put a ring on his finger and sandals on his feet. Bring the calf we have been fattening, and kill it; we are going to have a feast, a celebration, because this son of mine was dead and has come back to life; he was lost and is found.'

LUKE 15: 21–4

A JOURNEY INTO LOVE

After a mother has smiled for some time at her child, it will begin to smile back; she has awakened love in its heart, and in waking the child to love, she awakes also recognition. The sense impressions, at first empty of meaning, gather meaningfully round the 'thou'; the whole apparatus of knowledge and understanding comes into play with its power to perceive and to conceive because the play of love has been started by the child's mother. In the same way, God explains himself before man as love. Love radiates from God and instils the light of love in the heart of man: precisely a light in which he can perceive this – absolute – love.

H. U. VON BALTHASAR: *Love Alone*

Strange how helpless, compared with other species, the human baby is. Baby ducks slide down the bank and swim on their very first day; foals and calves can stand on their own feet only moments after they are born. But the human baby is utterly dependent, which is why, for me, the passage above is such a vivid description of the whole of man's journey into God. The embryonic spiritual life begins like that of a helpless baby capable only of very gradually responding to love. If only we could grasp this simple illustration – because the spiritual journey, the relationship with God in prayer is precisely this. If we can only understand that then all the pressure is off what we, mistakenly, imagine is something *we* must accomplish: it is not doing anything at all, it's responding to something that's done to us. 'Let it be done unto me' said one who hadn't the first clue what was happening to her.

[20]

While we are reflecting on the beginning of this journey, I think we should for a moment consider its ultimate goal. Where are we headed? The answer is in one word: love. Or rather in two words, absolute love. True, love *can* be a lightweight word squandered in every direction with no real meaning. But we cannot escape love, it is central to our existence. Love is where we all stand united on common ground, because there simply isn't a normal human being of any race, creed or colour who does not long to be truly loved, and truly love in return.

The problem is that somehow perfect love constantly eludes us, and subconsciously we settle for less than perfect love. So we (like Paul Simon) build fortresses and castles to protect ourselves from the pain of imperfect love and settle for affection, friendship or what Balthasar calls 'mutual islands of sympathy'. One of the most disturbing aspects of genuine self-discovery is the realisation that much, if not all, of what we thought was love has some element of self-motivation behind it. It's only in a relationship with God that we encounter pure, absolute and unconditional love.

I recall a friend of mine whose husband died suddenly realising, on being told of his death, that her first thoughts were for herself. What will happen to me? was her first instinct. It was a reaction that shocked her, yet these painful experiences of our own weakness in loving can be (if we let them) signposts pointing the way to pure love which is beyond ourselves. And because we all have that capacity for love – which is the sole purpose of our creation – we will inevitably feel the pain of that incompleteness and emptiness within that no created person can satisfy. Maturity consists in not settling for the shadows of finite love, but in learning how to receive that 'radiant light of life' that can instil itself in a heart open to receive it. We must stretch ourselves and dare to believe there really can be such fulfilment.

On that ancient exodus journey the Hebrews, after just one stage of their journey, were all ready to settle down right there on the other side of the Red Sea. But no, God had infinitely more to unfold for them: there was a promised land flowing with milk and honey, but their sights were not set high enough. They had to be lured to travel much further along the desert way. Love, infinite and unconditional love received and reciprocated, is the promised land at the end of *our* journey of prayer.

> *When you love you should not say 'God is in my heart' but rather 'I am in the heart of God' and think not that you can direct the course of love, for love if it finds you worthy directs your course.*
> *Love has no other desire but to fulfil itself.*
> *But if you love and must needs have desires let these be your desires:*
> *To melt and be like a running brook that sings its melody to the night.*
> *To know the pain of too much tenderness.*
> *To be wounded by your own understanding of love.*
> *And to bleed willingly and joyfully.*

KAHLIL GIBRAN: *The Prophet*

CHAPTER TWO

Will the Real God Please Stand Up?

THE LIFE-STIFLER GOD

I seek God! I seek God! He jumps in among the laughing crowd, pierces them with his glance and cries: 'Whither is God?' I will tell you. We have killed him, you and I. All of us are his murderers.

I suspect one of the major difficulties most of us have in our understanding of God is disentangling and discarding those received ideas of what he is like. He has suffered from what we might describe nowadays as a 'bad press'. We cannot help being coloured in our outlook by our earliest experiences of how God was first communicated.

Nietzsche's angry denial of the existence of God was surely due largely to his 'religious' upbringing in the moralistic atmosphere of the mid nineteenth century. The narrow-minded God whom he experienced had quite rightly to be killed off, so that the community of believers could be forced to redefine their distorted images in accordance with the first commandment: 'You shall have no gods except me'.

Unfortunately Nietzsche's god lives on, and still needs to be killed off again from time to time. He is the other-worldly one, bent on stifling human life, dead against pleasure or achievement: sensual pleasure is taboo, sexual pleasure not to be thought of. Eating is all right, so long as you don't enjoy the food too much; alcohol forbidden under any circumstances. He is not at all happy with success or creativity. In fact he is responsible for many people abandoning the practice of religion because he has convinced them that he only countenances

[25]

miserable worms. If you are to be counted among his elect, you just *have* to be materially impoverished.

The life-stifling god is at odds with human intellectual powers: he would suppress all science, philosophy, theology. His narrow fundamentalism makes it impossible even to consider how the evolution of the universe, far from denying the glory of its creator, rather enhances it. 'Keep 'em down' is his motto: if they get a chance to enjoy and achieve too much they will get out of hand.

We do need sometimes to reflect on some of our caricature gods if we are going to free ourselves from the distortions, in order to seek and ultimately know the real God. The God I know – the one who reveals himself in Scripture – is a far cry from the one described above. To echo Job, who was it who made earth and heaven? Who gave us the capacity to experience sensual pleasure? Who said 'go fill the earth and conquer it' (Genesis 1: 28), in other words grow, expand, develop? One of the dominant themes in the Scriptures is of God enjoying his people, and his people enjoying their God, and a recurrent image is that of the banquet, the wedding feast. Indeed it is one of the simplest yet most powerful descriptions of what the relationship between God and his people should be: a shared experience of joy and celebration (as every eucharist depicts in sign and symbol).

Let us hope Nietzsche's life-stifling god will one day be killed off for good, but it has not happened yet. One of his followers wrote to me once, during the transmission of a cookery series I was presenting, horrified to note that – as a Christian – I had given such a bad example to others by using wine in a recipe. Of course she knew the Scriptures, she added, and had read that famous line where Paul tells Timothy to 'take a little wine for his stomach' (1 Timothy 5: 23). But she assured me that what Paul had actually meant was (wait for it), to rub it on!

> *On this mountain the Lord will prepare*
> *for all peoples, a banquet of fine wines*
> *of food rich and juicy.*

On this mountain he will remove
the mourning veil covering all peoples.
He will destroy death for ever.
The Lord will wipe away the tears
from every cheek; he will take away
the people's shame everywhere on the earth.
That day it will be said,
See, this is our God.

ISAIAH 25: 6–9

THE GOD OF FEAR AND ANXIETY

Let me assert my firm belief that the only thing we have to fear is fear itself.

FRANKLIN D. ROOSEVELT

This is the god who lurks in your shadow and waits for you to make a mistake. I will always recall my first live cookery demonstration, seeing a fierce lady in the front row, arms folded: sure enough, she was there for no other reason than to point out my mistakes. In the end her very presence was enough to cause me to make mistakes! It was such a relief later on to be able to do all my demonstrating in front of uncritical television cameras.

This god has no understanding of human frailty, nor of circumstances or influences we cannot avoid. Perfection in All Things is his motto. He is quite often born in people's minds during the formative years as the embodiment of parents or teachers or people in authority: anyone who has been severely punished or pressured to see the world as a place where mistakes are not tolerated, is very susceptible to this god. I have a friend who still jokes about a dreaded figure called Father Murphy. Whenever he was naughty as a child his mother would ask 'Whatever would Father Murphy say if he could see you doing that?' So the god whom Father Murphy represented became some tyrant interested only in little boys' mistakes.

Perhaps the most difficult thing about banishing these caricature gods is that they still have their devoted followers. Literature is littered with these wrathful characters who cloak their perversion in counterfeit religion: Mr Barrett (of Wimpole Street) whose severity was projected in the name of God always, for me, epitomised this species. Thankfully hell-fire and damnation have all but disappeared from the pulpit nowadays — though I still have to pass a little chapel near our home, whose sign reminds me every day that 'The wages of sin is death'!

Fear, in my opinion, is the most inhibiting of human evils: it is indeed the only thing we have to fear in seeking a relationship with the real God. It is significant that, in the Scriptures, almost every encounter with God is prefaced with the words 'Do not be afraid'. The one thing we can be sure of in our groping for understanding is the truth of those words. For as the psalmist puts it 'He knows of what we are made' (Psalm 102/103). Who else but God, our creator, can understand — and make good — our human frailty? Who else can measure the circumstances that have caused bitterness, or pain, or longing?

It is precisely in all of this that he meets us, touches us. We have heard it before, but we always need to hear it more deeply: that the one lost, frightened person is of most concern to him than the ninety-nine that have reached perfection.

John the evangelist's famous line from his first letter states that perfect love is what drives out fear (1 John 4: 18). In prayer what we are doing essentially is allowing God to love us, learning how to receive, perhaps for the first time in our lives, the pure and unconditional love which comes to us as we are, where we are and drives away our fear.

> *You whom I brought from the confines of the earth*
> *and called from the ends of the world;*
> *You to whom I said, you are my servant,*
> *I have chosen you not rejected you.*
> *Do not be afraid, for I am with you;*
> *stop being anxious and watchful . . .*
> *for I your God am holding you by the right hand;*
> *I tell you, 'Do not be afraid. I will help you.'*

ISAIAH 41: 9, 10, 13

THE GOD OF THE WELL-INFORMED

Jesus said to them, 'Who do you say that I am?'
They replied 'You are the eschatological manifes-
tation of the ground of our being, the kerygma of
which we find the ultimate meaning in our inter-
personal relationships.' And Jesus said, 'What?'

GRAFFITI, ST JOHN'S UNIVERSITY,
NEW YORK

One modern American writer, Monika Hellwig, has described the twentieth-century version of the gospel story of Christ's cleansing of the temple. If he were here today, she said, he would be taking his whip cords and overthrowing some of the tables in the colleges of theology. What she meant was that in some cases theology was in danger of robbing the poor of the meaning of the Gospel. Not the physically poor, but the ordinary people who wish to understand the gospel teachings outside any formal theological training. For her, theology should serve the needs of the poor rather than deprive them.

The false god in all this is the one who requires you to have a doctorate in theology before you can seriously begin to know what he's about. The declension of Greek verbs takes precedence over the Sermon on the Mount. You'll need Hebrew and Latin, too, and a smattering of German if at all possible. He is somehow exclusive to the well-informed: lesser mortals have to make do with their own naive interpretations of the great truths of faith. His motto is never use a short word where a

long one will do (this is not exclusive to theology, by the way –
cookery writing also has its own superior practitioners).

I once stood in the middle of a vast library in a leading
theological college. Having already been through several
floors packed with row upon row of books, I felt quite
overwhelmed at the sheer weight of words around me. I
suppose I must have given some hint of this, for my guide, a
leading biblical scholar, turned and remarked rather poignantly how two thousand years of scholarship had whittled
away at the Gospels until there seemed to be hardly anything
left.

Of course, biblical and theological studies are vital, not only to
the Church but to the wider world in finding answers to secular
questions. They are something to be treasured, and we owe
much to those brave theologians whose critical function has
been to push at the frontiers of belief in order to give more, not
less, life and vitality to faith.

In the final analysis what we need is a balance between the dry
and pedantic treatises and the simplistic trivialised view. Our
real God communicates himself with profoundness *and* simplicity. While you can know all there is to know about the
teachings of theology and not know God, it is also true
that you can know God without knowing a single word of
theology.

> *Where there is the tree of knowledge, there is always
> paradise: so say the most ancient and the most
> modern serpents.*
> FRIEDRICH NIETZSCHE

THE GOD OF THE EXTRAORDINARY

He who believes himself to be far advanced in the spiritual life has not even made a good beginning.

One of the things that emerges from the history of the people of God is that those who have played a leading part in the formation of faith seem to have been the unlikeliest of people. God, it would appear, always uses the ordinary and unexceptional to communicate something of himself. Yet once again we have fashioned for ourselves a god who would operate in a totally opposite way.

This is the god of the extraordinary, an ethereal, other-worldly god who is not at all at home among ordinary people. This god has to be viewed with tongue firmly in cheek, yet he does cause great problems for people genuinely seeking faith. For anyone with a healthy sense of scepticism he is a total turn-off: but he can also do great damage to those who are conscientiously seeking truth. They can sometimes feel themselves to be second-class members of the human race because of their utter lack of any kind of the extraordinary religious experience which his followers seem to enjoy.

Some of his followers seem to feel the need, when speaking of him or addressing him directly in his heavenly enclave, to use a special kind of voice – usually an octave higher or lower than normal. I once heard one of his clan talking about the ordinary members of the parish being only able to understand things 'at pew level'. His kind are a select bunch who live on another plane altogether: they wear invisible badges which say 'I am chosen', and on the hot line to their god they are vouchsafed all sorts of secrets and special messages. Much time is taken up in visions and ecstasies and they very often wear themselves out with evangelising because their poor ineffectual god is in great need of all their efforts if he's going to save the world.

Sometimes there are macho moments, though. He's very good at signs and wonders, especially at rallies where loud cheering erupts as miracle after miracle is relayed over the loud-speakers. Now I'm not against a good miracle, now and then but en bloc they tend to get – dare I say it – somewhat trivial. I will never forget one lady at a prayer-meeting recounting divine intervention when she had forgotten to put a note out for extra milk. Lo and behold, the exact number of pints needed were waiting for her the next day!

The sad thing about this god is that he does offer a distraction and escape from the pains and problems of reality. Recently a nun of my acquaintance who had been working in Syria reported that a very holy woman in a local village had received the wounds of Christ on her body one particular Good Friday morning. The whole village turned out to witness the spec-tacle, and there were long queues waiting day and night to get a glimpse of the phenomenon. The danger with this and other forms of 'extraordinary' phenomena is that they can obscure the fact that really to be a Christian means learning how to see the wounds of Christ in those around us. We certainly don't need to queue all night; in fact most of us need look no further than our own families.

What betrays this god is his showiness. Like anything else religion *can* be merely an exercise in self-cultivation. But true holiness lies hidden in (and quite unknown to) the person who attains it. If we are bent upon the extraordinary, we miss out on the ordinary. We miss the real God who does not make his home in shrines and temples, but in the hearts of men.

> *How sad it is to see certain souls, like rich merchant ships, laden with good works, spiritual exercises, virtues and gifts of God which, because they cannot summon up the courage to break with certain tasks, attachments or affections, never reach the harbour of perfect union. Yet it would cost them but a single flight to break the thread that holds them.*

> ST JOHN OF THE CROSS: *Ascent and Mount Carmel*

THE GOD OF THE FIT AND STRONG

While he was at dinner in the house it happened that a number of tax collectors and sinners came to sit at the table with Jesus and his disciples. When the Pharisees saw this, they said to his disciples 'Why does your master eat with tax collectors and sinners?' When he heard this he replied, 'It is not the healthy who need a doctor but the sick. Go and learn the meaning of the words: "What I want is mercy not sacrifice". And indeed I did not come to call the virtuous but sinners.'

MATTHEW 9: 10–13

This god is probably the most complex of all the strange gods we've encountered so far, the caricature god of that multitude of people who feel they can never be good enough to be included in his circle. He is a god whose approval not only has to be earned by human effort but seems to be available only through sheer good fortune.

Your luck is in if you happen to be born in the right circumstances, let us say into a secure family so that you grow into a stable sort of person with a sunny disposition; if you can form good relationships, make a good marriage, produce stable children; if you are a fine upstanding member of the community. And so on. This god still has St Peter standing at the pearly gates, allowing in only those who have passed all the right tests.

Creator of all, though he is, he cruelly allows some people to be born into third-world shanty towns where perhaps teenage prostitution is the only means to a square meal. If the unavoidable circumstances of your life have bruised you, rendered you incapable of attaining the 'normal' standards of decency, then you are simply on this god's scrap-heap. Very well, that is an over-statement, but this god is so pervasive we need to see the lie for what it is.

He specialises in guilt and dishes out back-breaking burdens of it, so there is no choice but to run away from him in the hope that ignoring the load might in some way lighten it. Young people, in particular, are vulnerable to him, in that they may have been brought up with some kind of belief, yet as soon as they feel their moral lives are not quite of the order expected they stop going to church or praying. The fact is, of course, that this is when they are most in need of support and reassurance.

The god of the healthy demands that you get your own house in order first, then come back and practise your faith. His 'Church' has no room for hypocrites. 'Call yourself a Christian? Behaving in this way, or that, *and* going to church!'

Well why not, is something approaching the appropriate answer. The real God sits at table, invites the socially unacceptable to join him, and offers compassion. The root of the word is actually 'suffering' with, and that is what he offers: a side-by-side sharing of pain and difficulty and help in overcoming its causes. His answer to those finger-wagging followers of our false god is, go and find out what compassion is really all about, because that is what *I* am about.

> *We must learn to regard people less in the light of what they do or omit to do, but more in the light of what they suffer.*
>
> DIETRICH BONHOEFFER

THE CUDDLY-BEAR GOD

The atheist staring from his attic window is often nearer to God than the believer caught up in his own false image of god.

MARTIN BUBER

This is the god who provides all who follow him with rose-coloured spectacles, through which they 'see' only a narrow finite view of what tender love and mercy are about. His devotion means re-interpreting the Scriptures. For instance 'do not be afraid' means 'don't worry about a thing, do nothing'. This sweet-scented god of the cheap greetings cards and unctuous religious verses is falling over himself to smooth out all the ruffles of life. Through him you can switch off the pain of reality around you, and keep busy and smiling.

He sometimes acts as a kind of insurance policy with church attendance being the premium. It's quite a pleasant one too, provided it is quaint or 'traditional' enough not to offer any hint of a challenge: after all, the language in which the creed is recited is what's most important, the solemn declarations of belief are really optional extras.

His congregation can be like spoiled children, never challenged to grow into a greater experience of real life or real God. Their situation is summed up by Francis Thompson in his poem 'The Hound of Heaven' where though God pursues the soul, the soul resists 'lest having Him I must have naught beside'. The problem with the real God is that he might just want some kind of radical change of heart – not in lifestyle or in the material sense, but in facing up to realities. Locked inside a walled rose-garden, the cuddly-bear brigade can be in full control of what they should or should not do.

Their god is so understanding that absolutely everything goes. I once heard the sad story of a woman whose marriage had grown dull falling in love with someone who like her was a member of the local church. He too was in love with her, but there was no future for their relationship as he was married and anyway ambitious in his career which divorce might have damaged. In the event he was content to keep up a secret relationship, though she suffered intensely. His cuddly-bear god however 'understood' that neither of their marriages was satisfactory, that no one was getting hurt because no one knew, that there couldn't be anything wrong with *love* after all. She was not so convinced of these justifications, yet found herself unable to live without him. What is wrong with our cuddly-bear caricature is that, while he may not condone the situation, he is impotent to offer the help that could set them free.

This god stultifies that growth in spiritual life which, albeit slow and undetected, eventually enables a person to make decisions about his or her life in complete freedom. Mistakes happen and not every human need can be met in the way we feel perhaps it should be, but it is only the real God who sees our hidden reasons without condemnation and at the same time wants to take us past our self-justifications and beyond our dim and finite vision of what can in the end best fulfil us.

> *This then is what I pray, kneeling before the Father from whom every family whether spiritual or natural takes its name. Out of his infinite glory may he give you the power through his Spirit for your hidden self to grow strong ... Glory be to him whose power, working in us, can do infinitely more than we can ask or imagine.*

EPHESIANS 3: 14–17, 20

THE UNHOLY GOD

*And he showed me something small, no bigger than
a hazelnut, lying in the palm of my hand. I looked at
it and thought, what can this be? And I was given
this general answer: it is everything which is made. I
was amazed that it could last because it looked so
small and fragile.*
*And I was answered in my understanding. It lasts
and always will, because God loves it and everything has being through the love of God. In this little
thing I saw three things: God made it, God loves it,
and God cares for it.*

JULIAN OF NORWICH

The unholy god exists only by default. He is the product of
what happens when we lose sight of what holiness really
means. If you wish to plan a journey, obviously you need a
map; but the map is not much use unless you are aware of the
scale. One inch could represent one mile or a thousand,
depending on which map you are using. Equally on a spiritual
journey we need to reflect on the scale of the holiness of God.

Is he the all-powerful creator of everything seen and unseen? If
so, then clearly he lies beyond us: holy God, as one writer put
it, is 'wholly other' and our poor human concepts are inadequate to grasp the whole. But like Mother Julian with her
hazelnut, we can get an inkling. That tiny fragile thing she saw
in the palm of her hand immediately put her in touch with the
scale of God's absolute holiness and enveloping care for *all* of
creation.

When we lose our sense of awe and wonder at the wholly

otherness of God, we soon begin to distort the scale. We grow greater, and God grows smaller. We begin to know what should or should not be, we cultivate our own ideas of what a loving God is all about – *he* needs to be in the palm of *our* hand. If he really loved us there would not be wars, famines, earthquakes, child murders . . . Because he doesn't fit into our limited concepts, he is rendered ineffectual.

The unholy god (if he existed) would have made a puppet universe and simply pulled all the strings to keep everything orderly and peaceful. Those who want an unholy god who behaves in accordance with finite plans are really wanting a puppet existence for themselves, where there is no freedom, no choice, no understanding. In contrast the Holy God breathes life into people then waits and watches – like the biblical image of the mother eagle hovering over and nurturing her young, and taking them onto her outstretched wings until they are strong enough to fly up to the heavens on their own.

Evil is present where love is absent, and while the world gropes its way towards – is nurtured towards – that total love that is the purpose of its existence, it is constantly in conflict with that evil. One of the most moving witnesses to the holiness of God – and the rejection of an unholy god – came from the father of a twenty-year-old girl who had been killed by an IRA bomb at the Remembrance Day service in Enniskillen. They had both been trapped in the debris: she had died and he had lived. 'I can't help wondering why it wasn't me,' he said. 'Her life was only just beginning. Yet I know that God has a bigger plan for all of us. If I didn't believe that I would commit suicide.' Visibly and tragically bereaved, this man was able not only to forgive but continue to hope for something as yet unseen and beyond himself.

I know that you are all-powerful:
what you conceive, you can perform.
I am the man who obscured your designs
with my empty-headed words.
I have been holding forth on matters I cannot understand,
on marvels beyond me and my knowledge.

I knew you then only by hearsay;
but now, having seen you with my own eyes,
I retract all I have said,
and in dust and ashes I repent.

JOB 42: 2–3, 5–6

CHAPTER THREE

Through a Glass Darkly

THE UNTHINKABLE

To come to a knowledge you have not, you must come by a way you know not.

ST JOHN OF THE CROSS

What all those false images of God we've just been considering have in common is that they are all attempts to reduce the unthinkable down to the thinkable. What we then get is a god that is no more all-embracing than the limits of our imagination. To realise just how finite that is one only has to think how science has pushed the frontiers of the known universe out to trillions of light years away – and yet our galaxy is said to be only a tiny fragment. To try to imagine *all* that exists being as tiny and fragile as Mother Julian's hazelnut and held and sustained by a loving creator is self-evidently beyond our human powers of perception.

A graphic illustration of the failure of rational analysis is to be found in the Book of Job, where Job and his friends are grappling with the problem of suffering and trying to figure it out on an intellectual level. God's famous rebuke puts it delightfully into perspective: 'Where were you' he enquires of Job 'when I made the heavens and the earth?' Job gets the point: that his own impoverished imaginings are separated from the awesome holiness of God by an enormous gulf and yet . . . his instinctive cry from the heart for a true friend to share the burden of his suffering can find realisation *only* in the heart of God himself.

It is not only our reasoning, but our instinct too, that tells us that there is something 'other', something beyond, something

that we desire and hope will share the pain of our incompleteness, and provide our fulfilment. Only the atheist *knows* that
what can't be thought or imagined simply cannot be. Even the
agnostic shares with the true believer the awareness that the
search for God involves transcending our human faculties and
a willingness to reach beyond them. Faith, like life itself, is a
gift. We can't actually initiate it, but we can reach out for it and
receive it.

What faith really is, is a willingness to take on the mystery and
to travel the as yet unknown way. The journey can perhaps be
likened to entering a darkened room: your eyes accustomed to
the strong daylight outside will be temporarily blinded. Yet if
you are willing to wait a while, settle down for a period of time,
the eyes do eventually begin to adjust. They gradually become
more familiar with the surrounding darkness, and become
aware of shapes and forms. Eventually you can move around
the room freely without fear.

Faith then, as we have said, is not a blind venture but the
following up of an instinct that leads us to an understanding,
and although I can't think God with my mind I *can* know him
on that deeper spiritual level, that other level of my life which I
can accept and enter into. My own favourite scriptural image
of this knowing God in an unknown way is in the story of
Moses in the cave. In this life we know he's there, we are aware
of his passing by us in the midst of our daily round, but we
cannot as yet see the full extent of who and what he is.

> *And when my glory passes by, I will put you in a
> cleft of the rock and shield you with my hand while I
> pass by. Then I will take my hand away and you
> shall see the back of me; but my face is not to be
> seen.*
> EXODUS 33: 22–3

THE PEOPLE OF GOD

Believing that they are led by the spirit of the Lord who fills the whole earth, the people of God set out to discover among the events, needs and aspirations they share with contemporary man, what are the genuine signs of the presence and purpose of God. For faith sheds new light on everything and reveals the divine intention about man's entire vocation.

The Church in the Modern World

Although these words come from the opening chapter of the document describing the role of the modern Church in the world, as a statement of what it means to be a human being in search of God, I believe it has relevance for any age or generation. Granted that God will always be mystery, where does the search for him begin?

The answer is ironically simple: in his people. That is where he is present, and through them in all others as well. In the world, in the whole of creation and especially in people, faith comes to us through the lived human experience and more specifically through those whose lives have been centred on God, the whole community of believers. If your last experience of a church service led you to believe otherwise, let me straight-away explain that what we are trying to discern here is the presence of God among his own people throughout the whole of history. And throughout history this journey of discovery seems to have taken two directions.

The ancient philosophers – and their heirs – tried to arrive at knowledge of God through the powers of reason, through the commonsense assumption that the beauty and order of the universe must be the work of some divine creator. The other approach is the antithesis of that: the band of people who searched for God by way of faith (the first four words of the Bible are 'In the beginning God . . .') (Genesis 1: 1). The Jewish people began their journey with an instinctive belief that right in the beginning there was a God, availed themselves of his gratuitous gift of faith, and set out to discern his meaning and purpose in the whole of creation.

What the history of the Jews – and no less other major religions – illuminates is that a simple expectant belief draws people into a real experience of God in their daily lives. It is always a collective experience; from the dawn of history the quest for God is rooted in a pilgrim people bound together by their shared human experience, and what is revealed to the world is a collective consciousness of God's presence within them. My own favourite interpretation of the name 'Israel' (said to translate as 'God struggles') given to Jacob who wrestled with God until he blessed him, is an image of man's entire struggle for God and God's own struggle for man.

I find it awesome to look back at the history of this pilgrim people and see that, notwithstanding all the human frailties, mistakes and failures that punctuate their struggle, there does exist a unity and a vision of God that belongs not just to a privileged few but to a whole people – 'from age to age he gathers a people' – and yes, from this collective experience which spans history, we do indeed know what he is like. I share my own belief in God, and what he is like, with Abraham, with Isaiah, with Paul, Thomas More, Thérèse of Lisieux. My experience is linked to their experience, in the frailties and failures no less than the vision. They are mine too, but through them and what they have communicated, shared and handed down, we are all collectively struggling and feeling our way towards him, and since it is in him that we all 'live and move and have our being' He is not very far away, but dwelling within all human life, every race and nation. St Paul's words to the Greeks, as he wandered around looking at their man-made

shrines for worshipping man-made gods, expresses this reality
most profoundly:

> *So Paul stood before the whole Council of the*
> *Areopagus and made this speech: 'Men of Athens, I*
> *have seen for myself how extremely scrupulous you*
> *are in all religious matters, because I noticed, as I*
> *strolled round admiring your sacred monuments,*
> *that you had an altar inscribed: To An Unknown*
> *God. Well, the God whom I proclaim is in fact the*
> *one whom you already worship without knowing it.*
> *Since the God who made the world and everything*
> *in it is himself Lord of heaven and earth, he does not*
> *make his home in shrines made by human hands.*
> *Nor is he dependent on anything that human hands*
> *can do for him, since he can never be in need of*
> *anything; on the contrary, it is he who gives every-*
> *thing – including life and breath – to everyone.*
> *From one single stock he not only created the whole*
> *human race so that they could occupy the entire*
> *earth, but he decreed how long each nation should*
> *flourish and what the boundaries of its territory*
> *should be. And he did this so that all nations might*
> *seek the deity and, by feeling their way towards him,*
> *succeed in finding him. Yet in fact he is not far from*
> *any of us, since it is in him that we live, and move,*
> *and exist, as indeed some of your own writers have*
> *said: "We are all his children".'*
>
> ACTS 17: 22–8

GOD AS WORD

Yes, as the rain and snow come down from the heavens and do not return without watering the earth, making it yield and giving growth to provide seed for the sower and bread for the eating, so the word that goes from my mouth does not return to me empty, without carrying out my will and succeeding in what it was sent to do.

ISAIAH 55: 10–11

Sooner or later in addressing the question 'How can we know what God is like?' we have to consider his own account of himself as revealed within the writings of Scripture, and in the context of the people of faith who not only wrote down their experiences and inspirations, but also preserve and communicate the teachings contained in them.

So how does God speak? Through 'sources close to . . .' to borrow an analogy from the newspapers for a moment. Prayer, as we shall see over and over again, is a relationship and people who relate to God are coming closer to him. In this closeness God imparts his wisdom – not just for the person concerned but for everyone. All through history there have been people whose relationship with God has enabled them to speak prophetically to the rest of the world. These deliverers of God's word are not in themselves special – in fact in the Bible they often appear to be the most unwilling of spokesmen. Their role is only relevant in the wider context of community, and the word only authentic in its productivity, in carrying out 'what it is sent to do' which is to turn the hearts of people towards him.

[50]

Somehow, in a way we cannot fathom, God's word is creative. That is the very first thing that the Bible reveals to us – in the powerful imagery of the first chapter of Genesis. At the very beginning we are presented with a vision of God's spirit hovering over darkness and chaos. There is nothing, until he speaks, and in the same moment that he speaks the word ('Let there be light' (Genesis 1: 13), light appears. All creation is the response to – the realisation if you like – of the spoken word of God.

In the Old Testament this creative word is communicated on many different levels, not just through the medium of patriarchs and prophets: but perhaps more importantly it is transmitted in the stories of ordinary people in the events of everyday life. God speaks his word through their limited experience, both in relationship to himself and to each other. And their experiences speak to us in just the same way; their human reactions absolutely mirror our own peaks of fervour and troughs of doubt. What we see and hear in the Scriptures are very human stories about very ordinary people, whose struggles are precisely like ours. Moses' encounter with the presence of God in the burning bush filled him with wonder and awe but when he came to approach the dreaded Pharaoh with a message from God his faith failed him as he uttered a whole string of protests!

As we read and begin to hear the stories of the people of God in Scripture, we begin to understand and share their experiences and in this way the word of God begins to permeate our own life. By doing this we are allowing the word to be creative.

Perhaps an appropriate way to end this reflection would be to read chapter one of Genesis, not as a study but purely as an exercise in listening and responding to what are in fact some of the most beautiful words in Scripture. They may or may not provide a springboard for thought about this vast creation we are part of: the important thing is not to anxiously analyse if there is meaning to the words, but to relax with them. If they send you to sleep – you probably need a sleep, so even that is creative!

For Wisdom is quicker to move than any motion:
she is so pure, she pervades and permeates all things.
She is a breath of the power of God,
pure emanation of the glory of the Almighty;
hence nothing impure can find a way into her.
Although alone, she can do all;
herself unchanging, she makes all things new.
She makes them friends of God and prophets.

WISDOM 7: 24–5, 27

GOD AS FATHER

When Israel [my people] was a child I loved him,
and I called my son out of Egypt.
But the more I called to them, the further they
  went from me . . .
I myself taught Ephraim to walk,
I took them in my arms.
Yet they have not understood that I was the one
  looking after them.
I led them with reins of kindness,
with leading strings of love.
I was like someone who lifts an infant close
  against his cheek;
stooping down to him I gave him his food.

HOSEA 11: 1–4

Because God is manifest in all of human existence, to learn about him we need to begin by looking no further than at ourselves. In our own loving human relationships, we can get glimpses of God's all-embracing relationship with us. We can only glimpse it because our own experiences only illuminate one aspect of his relationship with us at a time: where we relate to others specifically as father or mother, friend or lover, God is each of these as well as all of these to us.

That is why the current controversy within the feminist movement about the 'masculine' bias in the Scriptures and the Church's liturgy has its pitfalls. While we owe a debt to the movement for highlighting the feminine aspects of God, there is a danger in extreme cases of distorting the balance and losing our grip on the masculine. 'Let us make man in our own image

– in the image of God . . . Male and female he created them' (Genesis 1: 26). That verse from the first chapter of Genesis has it in a nutshell: both male and female sexuality express something of God. We ourselves are made up of a finely balanced selection of male and female hormones, and just as we need to experience both the masculine and feminine in our lives, so we have the same need in our approach to an understanding of God. Sexuality means separateness, incompleteness. In God we see the completeness and harmony of male and female that we ourselves look forward to.

So let us begin with the recurring biblical theme of God as father. What first of all are the attributes of a loving, caring father? Strength, protection, the ability to provide for his family, to offer security and freedom from anxiety. A loving father will, at the same time, impose a certain discipline that is tempered by knowledge and foresight rooted in love.

The image of paternal love is dominant in the passage quoted at the beginning of Hosea. A few verses further on we hear that, although his children have not understood that he was looking after them and have been disloyal and unfaithful, yet it is a father's love that prevails over his anger: 'How could I part with you . . . how could I give you up . . . My heart recoils from it, my whole being trembles at the thought' (Hosea 11: 8). A father figure indeed, whose love is unconditional and whose compassion will never be withheld.

Pure love though cannot impose itself, and I'm sure there is no better allegory of this aspect of fatherhood in the whole of Scripture than in the story of the prodigal son. It is his father's love that permits the son his freedom, even though that freedom leads to disaster. In his quest for independence, however, he has not forfeited that love. Even when he was 'still a long way off' his father runs down the road to greet him back, clasp him in his arms and hold him close.

In our journey of prayer it is normal and natural to be uncomprehending in the face of the mysterious truths of God, but we are not left absolutely in the dark, we are at least given these simple human images to reflect on. Of course there can be a problem here if my own personal experience of a father's love is flawed and inadequate, but in prayer I can at least begin to grasp how it is meant to be and even more than that, prayer puts me on the receiving end of a father's perfect and absolute love, where I can begin to experience perhaps for the first time what providence, protection, foresight and loving discipline are really about. The word father is in fact a rather formal translation of the Hebrew *Abba*, which might really be better rendered as 'daddy'. The relationship we are invited to share is a close and familiar one, and our part in this relationship is to respond and learn to entrust ourselves to this divine father-hood, in other words to become in spirit like a little child relating to a very loving daddy.

> *The word 'Father' is full of feeling, warm with affection. This revises the natural vision of God. How fatal if we see God as infinite monotony, aloof, self-absorbed. But God is fire, in him there is heat, and heart and desire. Desire to inflame and rekindle and recreate things numbed by dread of divinity. We cannot see the Father, the light is too strong. Yet we are drawn to him as moths to a candle and cannot end this ache by substitutes, by men or women or money. The Father is the universal future, the mag-net of all mankind.*

HUGH LAVERY: *Reflections on the Creed*

GOD AS MOTHER

This fair and lovely word 'Mother' is so sweet and so
kind in itself that it cannot be said of anyone or to
anyone except of him and to him who is the true
mother of life and of all things. To the property of
motherhood belong nature, love, wisdom and
knowledge, and this is God. For though it may be
so that our bodily bringing to birth is only little,
humble and simple in comparison with our spiritual
bringing to birth, still it is he who does it in the
creatures by whom it is done. The kind, loving
mother who knows and sees the need of her child
guards it very tenderly as the nature of motherhood
will have.

JULIAN OF NORWICH

All through the Scriptures we can find the imagery of the
paternal providence and wisdom of God complemented by
the feminine attributes of motherhood: softness, tenderness,
nurturing love. What is repeatedly expressed through the
prophetic word is God's profound involvement with all
aspects of motherhood: in a literal sense every human life is
'born of God'. Thus the psalmist: 'Yes, it was you who took me
from the womb, entrusted me to my mother's breast. To you I
was committed from my birth, from my mother's womb you
have been my God' (Psalm 21/22: 10).

The typically Jewish adage that 'God created mothers because
he couldn't be everywhere at once' almost expresses the
mystery that all earthly motherhood is a spiritual surrogate: 'It
is he who does it' as Julian says. And as the maternal relationship develops, so does the spiritual one. Through the

words of Isaiah we hear God's guarantee: 'Does a mother forget her baby or fail to cherish the child of her womb? Even if these forget, I will never forget you' (Isaiah 49: 15).

However imperfect the human mother–child relationship is, God is our truest and closest mother. We may not understand, see or feel this reality, but like a baby whose eyes are tightly closed suckles instinctively at the breast, so we are unknowingly embraced and nurtured throughout the whole of our lives.

Without exception, there is a child deep within all of us whose need is most of all for the maternal gift of tenderness that soothes away all our distress. Is this not what babies cry out for – and is it not what all humanity cries out for in its pain and confusion? Is it not why people get drunk or reach for the tranquillisers? I am reminded of a powerful scene in a play called *Road*, where four young unemployed victims of our urban dereliction find themselves in a crumbling condemned house. Two of them are men and two are women, and part of their problem, added to their social disadvantages, involves the loneliness of sexuality and pressures of role-playing. The men are expected to act a part, to be tough and macho, while the women feel they have to be sex objects. They are brought to the point of sharing their anger and frustration, and one of the men offers his anaesthetising solution: first he invites each one to drink a whole bottle of wine – straight down – then as the effects of the alcohol begin to permeate, he plays a special piece of music. It is the 1960s version of Otis Redding singing his emotionally-charged rendering of 'Try a Little Tenderness'. Suddenly, and *most* profoundly, it makes the point. Tenderness is what is actually absent from their wretched lives, and somehow the shared realisation of this gives them communion with each other and together they dimly perceive some hope for the future.

Prayer, as a relationship with God as Mother, puts us in touch with tenderness at the very deepest level. It is here that we gradually learn first and most importantly how to be tender with ourselves and then how to extend that tenderness to others — not as superficial reassurances but as a genuine reaching-out to another in understanding and acceptance.

> *And you shall suck, you shall be carried upon her hip and dandled on her knees. As one whom his mother comforts so will I comfort you. You shall be comforted in Jerusalem. You shall see, and your heart shall rejoice.*
>
> ISAIAH 66: 12–14

GOD AS FRIEND

His conversation is sweetness itself,
he is altogether lovable.
Such is my Beloved, such is my friend.

SONG OF SONGS 5: 16

In the very opening chapters of the Bible we are offered a prospect of God's intended friendship with us. The vision is of him as companion to Adam and Eve, sharing their existence in a carefree paradise, walking side by side with them in the cool of the evening. But the vision becomes clouded because of their disloyalty to this friendship: in shame Adam and Eve find it necessary to hide away from him. For us the journey back into this intimate friendship involves a choice, a free decision on our part to gradually come out of hiding.

The friendship of God is perhaps a harder notion to come to terms with than that of mother and father. A God, albeit bound to me by parental love, can still be kept at a safe distance: a true friend is another matter. Friendship implies a certain intimacy and commitment, but I suspect that one of the greatest difficulties we have in such a relationship with God is a feeling of inadequacy. With God at a distance I can live well enough with the darker side of myself: but if he comes too close what will happen then? What will be exposed?

This distancing is very much in evidence in human relationships – we fear that if people come close enough to know us intimately, they won't want to! There is a paradox here of course, because at the same time we long for intimate friendship, to be known as we really are. The problem is we are

A Journey into God

so often bruised by failed relationships, and lack of real acceptance, trust that is betrayed, fairweather friends who disappear at the first sign of trouble. Deep down we blame ourselves for not being all we think we should be.

What God offers in the Scriptures is friendship that touches and heals the darker side of humanity. I love Isaiah's reaction when, praying one day in the temple, he has a vision of God and he *feels*, as we all would, the terrible measure of his own inadequacy when confronted with holiness. 'What a wretched state I am in! I am lost, for I am a man of unclean lips and I live among a people of unclean lips' (Isaiah 6: 5). He wants quite understandably to cut and run, just as we would at such a close encounter. Faith is needed to believe that what God did for Isaiah he can do for us, more gradually perhaps, for we need the time to grow in the experience of his friendship before allowing him to come really close.

The journey of prayer is very much this journey into friendship, and we can take heart from many instances in the Scriptures where people's responses to God's friendship have been reassuringly human – incredulous, uncomprehending, sometimes even humorous. I rather like Gideon's reply to the angel of the Lord appearing to him in the days when Israel was oppressed by a foreign power. 'The Lord is with you, valiant warrior', to which Gideon's response is on the lines of 'Pardon me, Lord, but if that's so how come we're in the mess we're in now?' (Judges 6: 13). Even more amusing is God's promise that Gideon himself will lead the people out of captivity. Not he! Not the least important member of the weakest clan in Israel!

Do we not hear echoes of ourselves in that reaction? God can work his miracles in others, but never in me. Gideon needed a great deal of proof, but God is patient with his lack of faith, and ultimately Gideon does triumph over the oppressors. It is a lesson we all need to learn on our spiritual journey, that our own human frailties and weakness are never ever an obstacle in our relationship with God. He accepts us in true friendship totally as we are, where we are, and there won't be any surprises.

> For *without words, in friendship, all thoughts, all desires, all expectations are borne and shared with joy that is unacclaimed. And in the sweetness of friendship let there be laughter and a share of plea- sures. For in the dew of little things the heart finds its morn and is refreshed.*

KAHLIL GIBRAN: The Prophet

GOD AS LOVER

Set me as a seal on your heart,
Like a seal on your arm.
For love is strong as death,
Passionate love as relentless as death.
The flash of it is a flash of fire
A flame of God himself.
Love no flood can quench, nor torrent drown.

SONG OF SONGS 8: 6–7

Perhaps the totality of God's love for his creatures finds its pivotal expression in what we understand as passionate love, that of a lover for the beloved – and this is how it is depicted in both the Book of Hosea and in the Song of Songs. Beyond that, in both the Judaic and Christian traditions, the loving union of man and woman has constantly been presented as a symbol of the desired union between God and humanity. All of human life is a movement towards this union, which is the sole purpose of our existence.

In Hosea the scenario goes something like this: God compares his creatures to an unfaithful wife – worse, to a prostitute – who takes many lovers, seeking through them to provide for herself without her husband's help. The husband's anger blazes at such infidelity, but such is his love he cannot bring himself to give her up. He has the power to cut her off from her lovers, make her life barren, but the bitterness of that is not a punishment; it is the means of coaxing her back to her husband, the only one who will be a true and faithful lover to her.

In this simple story we can trace the unfolding of the love story between God and his people. Individually and collectively we too try to fulfil our deepest longings by our own efforts, flitting from lover to lover, seeking satisfaction in relationships, money, possessions, achievements, power. Yet for everyone time begins to run out: we find age creeping on, there are no more horizons and all that promise of fulfilment seems to be slipping away. But that emptiness and disillusion are the very things that can point us back towards the only source of fulfilment. 'She will chase after her lovers but not catch them, and then she will say "I will go back to my first husband . . ." She never realised that I was the one' (Hosea 2: 9).

God's total love supersedes death because it is eternal. Occasionally we can be permitted an insight into this truth: I remember standing by a graveside on a bitterly cold February day, my arm linked with an old man whose wife had suddenly been taken from him after a short illness. As the coffin was lowered he clung to me so tightly that I myself somehow experienced in that grief the power of his love for her, and understood that that grave and that coffin were only peripheral to it.

Even in its fullest sense the love of man and woman can only be a faint shadow of God's love for each and all his creatures, a love of such passionate intensity that death is no barrier. The depiction of God in the Scriptures as our lover has become a central theme of the spiritual journey for successive generations ever since (which is why the Song of Songs – essentially an allegory of courtship between two lovers – has been included in the canon of Scripture). The culmination of courtship is union, two beings becoming one flesh – not just physically, but bonded by love and commitment.

Great spiritual writers like St John of the Cross and Teresa of Avila have described the destination of the spiritual journey as 'spiritual marriage', a state where God takes full possession of a person. These are lofty notions and not easily comprehended, but in a letter written to St Thérèse of Lisieux by her sister there is a genuine perception of it. Responding to a description by Thérèse outlining her own spirituality (which she calls her 'little way') her sister Marie writes: 'Oh, I was very close to weeping as I read the lines that were not of this earth, but an echo from the heart of God. May I tell you? I will: you are *possessed* by God, literally possessed.'

St Paul in his letter to the Ephesians describes it as being 'filled with the utter fullness of God' (Ephesians 3: 19). My own interpretation is that full union with God is being filled with the fullness of love, where the self-centred ego has disappeared because love has replaced it.

> *Throughout the pages of the Old Testament with its history of humans as they really are – sinful, blind, obstinate, hard of heart – there shine stars, 'friends of God', who in some measure attained or were granted intimacy with the awful mystery. Such intimacy is still possible. Amidst a perverse and corrupt people 'Enoch walked with God; and he was not, for God took him' (Genesis 5: 24). Here, it is suggested, was someone for whom God meant so much that he was swallowed up by him. Enoch disappeared, only God shone out. In this pregnant phrase of scripture we have a summing up of holiness, of the perfection of human life.*

RUTH BURROWS: *Our Father*

CHAPTER FOUR

The History of a Promise

THE FIRST LESSON IN LOVE

*Choose life, then, so that you and your descendants
may live in the love of the Lord your God, obeying
his voice, clinging to him, for in this your life
consists.*

DEUTERONOMY 30: 20

In the opening chapters of Genesis the drama of the creation is
set before us, beautifully and poetically. As it unfolds – the
heavens, the earth, the plants, the birds of the air, the fish of the
sea, the animals of the earth – it is hard not to be drawn into the
excitement and expectancy of new life and all its potential. Of
God's creation of human beings 'in his image and likeness' we
are given two moving accounts. We read of God breathing his
own life-giving breath into his creatures, his gift of life shared
with each other, with the earth, and with God. Before creation
there is nothing, a formless void and a deep darkness; but what
creation initially enjoys is harmony and relationship with God,
man and woman above all for they are given the whole earth.
'Be fruitful, multiply, fill the earth and conquer it. . . *I will give
you all* . . .' (Genesis 1: 28).

It is a quite stunning offer. But in addition to this inheritance
they also have something else, they have the freedom to make
choices. This freedom (which their offspring will inherit) will
lead to mistakes, wrong choices and setbacks. Equally, as they
learn to understand this freedom, they will also have the
capacity to make the right choices. The root of their problem is
love, and the difficulties this presents.

What the stories in Scripture reveal as they unfold is an
account of God's love affair with the human race. At the outset

mankind is given a glimpse of the goal of this relationship: the Garden of Eden is symbolic of a place of total fulfilment and happiness. God's plan for his new-born universe is that love is the centre of its meaning. He could, in theory, have wanted a universe solely for beauty but no, he created it in love and entirely for love. But love if it is to be fulfilled will always seek reciprocation: the journey may be many-layered, but the achievement of it is total – the total gift of self to another. Again, God could have created a puppet universe that reciprocated love at the tug of a string. But that would not have been *true* love, because the freedom of choice would be absent.

Could we then be left free and not reciprocate? No, because life has no other meaning; love is its wellspring and creation can *only* be fulfilled in the final consummation of love. Death can only in the end be overcome by love. God's work with humanity is to coax it into making this choice. The way I see it is this: though we're free not to choose, in the end we will. I have often wanted to add a further sentence to the creed 'We believe in God – *and he believes in us*'. We will all come around to love in the end and accept God's offer of shared existence simply because ultimately we will finally understand the full implications of the alternative, the life or death of the whole of creation.

Back in the Garden the first test of love proved a disaster: the man and woman choose not to respond. Instead they choose to place themselves outside this intimate relationship, which like any relationship makes certain demands of fidelity. This mistake exposes them to the reality of pain and death, and they now have to begin the long slow journey back to life and learn the lessons of loving. They have to begin to learn how to choose God's life and love, how to obey his voice, how to cling to him and know that only in this clinging does their life consist.

> *I desired often to know what was our Lord's meaning. And fifteen years after and more, I was answered in inward understanding, saying, 'Would you know your Lord's meaning in this? Learn it*

*well. Love was his meaning. Who showed it you?
Love. What did he show you? Love. Why did he
show you? For love. Hold fast to this, and you shall
learn and know more about love, but you will never
need to know or understand about anything else for
ever and ever.' Thus did I learn that love was our
Lord's meaning.*

JULIAN OF NORWICH: *Enfolded in Love*

THE POSSIBILITY OF DEATH

The enigma of the human condition becomes greatest when we contemplate death. Man suffers not only from pain or the slow breaking down of his body, but also from the terror of perpetual extinction. It is a sound instinct that makes him recoil and revolt at the thought of this total destruction, of being snuffed out. He is more than matter, and the seed of eternity he bears within him rebels against death . . . While all imagination fails us in the face of death, the Church appeals to revelation in telling man that he is created for a blessedness beyond the wretchedness of this life.

The Church in the Modern World

One might be tempted to think, in this modern technological age, that atheism would appear to be a more plausible stance to most people than any specific belief in God or the hereafter, but polls and surveys of such attitudes actually reveal a different picture. They show a very low percentage of declared atheism. I'm sure that for most of the time people can sublimate the whole question of death as somehow having no immediate relevance, yet we continue to betray our anxiety in many subtle and perhaps unconscious ways. Is this not why people are preoccupied with health diets or aerobics or jogging, with hair restoration or facial surgery (alas necks and hands are always the sure giveaways!)? Each one a little 'victory' over the ageing process and, by implication, death itself.

We live after all in a world that perpetually teems with life, of plants and animals regenerating, babies being born, diseases overcome. One of the most vivid impressions that stays imprinted on my memory is a visit to the lowest point of the earth's surface, the Dead Sea: it was a most disquieting experience to come into contact with a space that contained no life whatsoever, and one I shan't forget. Yes, it is a sound instinct, our revolt against the antithesis of life, and a quite normal and natural one, in that we were created for life.

When the nineteenth-century atheists raged against God it was on the grounds that *he* was the life-stifler, that only human autonomy unfettered from his oppression could promote the real 'life experience'. But the consequences of this euphoric freedom from the idea of a God was that it led to nihilism, the death of everything. Perhaps that's why the polls show little enthusiasm now for atheism: remove the idea of God and you are in practice left with a void and a lack of meaning, a world without a soul.

The atheists attacked the preaching of eternal damnation as a threat to force people into religious submission, and fair enough for that was a dehumanising denial of any kind of freedom which has to be the prerequisite of any kind of loving. But the stark alternative they offered was another kind of hell, a dead sea containing no God and therefore no life. It is a possibility we have to consider and weigh up: that the human race could in theory reject God's love and end in death and annihilation. But there is another possibility – indeed a promise – against which we can balance it: that we do indeed carry the seed of eternity within, and hopefully as our journey unfolds we can begin to understand the remoteness of their kind of hell.

The words below were written by Friedrich Nietzsche, an atheist who proclaimed 'the death of God' but who perhaps understood and foresaw the consequences better than anyone.

What were we doing when we unchained this earth from its sun? Whither is it moving now? Whither are we moving? Away from all suns? Are we not plung-

ing continually? Backward? Sideward, forward in all directions? Is there still any up and down? Are we not straying through an infinite nothing? Do we not feel the breath of empty space? Has it not become colder? Is not night continually closing in on us?

THE PROMISE OF LIFE

I will shower blessings on you, I will make your descendants as many as the stars of heaven and the grains of sand on the seashore . . . All the nations of the earth shall bless themselves by your descendants as a reward for your obedience.

GENESIS 22: 17, 18

Alongside our very natural resistance to the idea of death there lies an equally fundamental desire that life should develop and expand. In a word, that it should be eternalised. It is this sound instinct that inspires the human urge to know God, and it is also this that has enabled people to be open and respond to a relationship with him.

To find our model for this response, one that epitomises both the individual response and the collective, we can go back to the earliest chronology of Scripture: to Abraham, who as the founding father of Judaism, Christianity and Islam is the patriarchal figure of a large section of today's believing world. In his life we see a relationship with God emerging, in which God is the initiator and all Abraham is required to do (in the early stages) is respond to that initiative by allowing himself to be led into unknown territory.

Abraham does respond, and God begins to make some extraordinary promises – the first of a series of promises that will form a thread throughout the Old Testament where 'I will give you . . .' will be a recurrent theme. The promises have far wider implications than simply Abraham himself: '*All* the nations of the earth will bless themselves by you.' Abraham does not comprehend the scale of these promises, nevertheless he devotes his life to living in the awareness of the presence of God. He builds altars and makes sacrifices to remind himself of the reality of this presence. God reciprocates by granting Abraham a tangible token of his presence, a longed-for son for his wife Sarah whose child-bearing years were long over.

As Abraham begins to understand the power of God, so his faith also grows until such time as it will stand the ultimate test of love. This is the point at which his commitment to the relationship is such that he can yield totally, even to the most painful demands which can be met with a love entirely devoid of self. Abraham agrees to sacrifice what means most in the world to him, the beloved son of his old age. Because of Abraham's self-giving Isaac is set free, but even more powerful than the dramatic story is its implications and insight into the truth that what overcomes death is love.

One of the Hebrew translations of the name Abraham is 'Father of the Pagans'. He was, in effect, one man and every man. The response to God was his, the fruits of it – God's initial promise – was for the whole universe: not just the Jewish or Christian community, but the community of the world. This is the thrilling thing, that God can intervene in a person's life, raise them up as he did with Abraham to the very perfection of love, but this will always be for the sake of others. Union with God becomes communion; community is shared unity. God's promise to Abraham is quite startling – blessings showered down upon his descendants through the generations until they reach *all* nations! Salvation history is under way, and the journey from death to life has begun.

> *Now that I am old and grey-headed,*
> *do not forsake me, God.*
> *Let me tell of your power to all ages,*
> *praise your strength and justice to the skies,*
> *tell of you who have worked such wonders.*
> *O God, who is like you?*
> *You have burdened me with bitter troubles,*
> *but you will give me back my life.*

You will raise me from the depths of the earth.
You will exalt me and console me again
so I will give you thanks on the lyre
for your faithful love, my God.

PSALM 70/71: 18–22

EXODUS AND
RELATIONSHIP

The sons of Israel, groaning in their slavery, cried
out for help, and from the depths of their slavery
their cry came up to God.
God heard their groaning and he called to mind his
Covenant.

EXODUS 2: 23–4

Throughout this book prayer has been characterised as a journey, and the milestones on this spiritual journey can conveniently be symbolised, as they are in the Scriptures, by familiar human concepts. Thus the journey is one from darkness to light, from death to life or – if we were to draw a parallel with that famous great biblical journey, the Exodus – from slavery to freedom. The analogy can be a very illuminating one, for what happened to the Hebrews is re-enacted, as it were, spiritually in every individual person's quest for God.

Both journeys, theirs and ours, occur within the context of what I consider to be the most important word of all in regard to prayer, relationship. But at the outset the Hebrew people are isolated from this relationship with their God. Note that their *circumstances* were no fault of their own. They had been born into a condition of slavery and oppression from which they could see no prospect of freeing themselves. They were denied even the practice of their religion, unable to celebrate, or relate to, the God of their ancestors. Their fate epitomises all who are cut off from God through the painful circumstances of their lives, and this predicament conjures up for me a mental picture of one of Francis Bacon's powerful paintings, which is to be found not far from my home in the Sainsbury Collection in the University of East Anglia. The painting depicts the twisted distorted image of a man, a slave, a prisoner of human pain and suffering, utterly unable to raise himself from the floor. How powerfully it speaks of the Hebrew slaves and the mental captivity of so much of the human condition, utterly unable to raise itself.

Though the Hebrew slaves were trapped and impotent they *were* able to do one thing – and that was cry for help. They remembered the God of their ancestors and his promise, and they ask him to set them free. It is precisely here that the inner journey of prayer begins, with a desire, a desire for freedom. They don't as yet know this God to whom they are appealing, but nonetheless they cry out from the very depths of their slavery. What they do soon discover is that his promise was indeed for all generations, and that his answer to their cry and his intervention in their lives could hardly have been more dramatic. The exodus journey begins with the famous crossing of the Red Sea, which is symbolic and a key event in the history of God's relationship with his people, its impact was such that it lives on still in the minds of both Jews and Christians: today each Christian baptism is a commemoration of this parting of the waters and a symbol of the embarking on a journey from death to life.

But like baptism, the crossing was not an end in itself. It is only an invitation to begin a journey on which they (and we) will learn to know and relate to their Deliverer. They, like us, were a motley bunch, weak, headstrong, full of complaints and ingratitude, and too often lacking in belief and trust. Yet there is still an inspiration in their story, because all the time God *was with them*, leading them, teaching them, infinitely patient.

In prayer we set out in precisely the same way, travelling a vast wilderness where we are not sure of our footing, where we have to learn how to surrender completely to another and be on the receiving end. Let's never underestimate how very difficult this is. Like the Hebrews we too are headstrong and want to do our own thing, believing all the time that we *will* receive all we need, and learning how to understand and recognise who it is who provides for us and carries us.

The crossing of the Red Sea was what can in modern times be called a born-again experience – but the people had to learn to move on from that into a real relationship, and hunger and thirst in the desert, bearing the daily dissatisfactions and failures of life. How easy it is to relate to a God up there in his heavens when the sun is streaming through the stained glass windows and all is well with the world, but it is on the less comfortable part of the journey that real relationship begins.

> *Do not take fright, do not be afraid of your enemies.*
> *The Lord your God goes in front of you and will*
> *fight on your side as you saw him fight in Egypt. In*
> *the wilderness too you saw him: how the Lord your*
> *God carries you as a man carries his child, all along*
> *the road you travelled.*
>
> DEUTERONOMY 1: 29–31

THE COVENANT

Hear, O Israel: the Lord your God is one Lord; and
you shall love the Lord your God with all your
heart, and with all your soul, and with all your
might. And these words which I command you this
day shall be upon your heart; and you shall teach
them diligently to your children, and shall talk of
them when you sit in your house, and when you
walk by the way, and when you lie down, and when
you rise.

DEUTERONOMY 6: 4–7

The biblical account of the Exodus is presented as a human
and very often touching story, of how a poor wretched band of
people are courted by God into a close relationship with
himself, one which ultimately will lead them towards the
fulfilment of their deepest needs. But, as we have already said,
it is also an illuminating allegory of the spiritual journey – and
on that level we can see it purely and simply as a journey of
trust.

Our problems differ very little from theirs. Looking out onto
that vast and empty desert – a relationship with a God I can
neither touch or see – we can easily recognise their human
reaction of panic. Where's the water coming from? Or the
food? To entrust ourselves to another and hang around waiting to receive! What if I don't? What if nothing happens?
Through all their various problems and setbacks in the end it
comes down to one thing, the decision to make a commitment
– this relationship which in biblical terms is to enter into the
covenant.

The root meaning of the biblical word for covenant is said to lie in the word 'fetter' or perhaps more precisely 'bonding'. I think a graphic way of describing this would be the three-legged race on a school sports day. Two people bound together and running as one. The covenant then is an invitation to become tied up with God in a side-by-side sharing of existence and the expression of this mutual bonding is love. For their part the people can only grasp this love if they, to put it simply, learn how to allow it to happen to them. In the material expression of this love – the parting of the sea, the water from the rock, the sending of the manna – they can gradually begin to learn that what is not humanly possible *is* possible at God's level. However barren the desert, somehow they do receive all they need. Having experienced this loving providence from God they then have to decide to commit themselves to responding to God's love for all time. The commandment to love is the key commandment and yet this all encompassing love of God is what seems to be so impossible on the human level. So it is, outside the context of a commitment. Love begins with a commitment to someone whom I then learn to love in the context of relationship. This response involves trustfully and willingly obeying God's commandments – which when all is said and done were an extremely socially acceptable list of what was most conducive to a healthy community life!

In the text of Deuteronomy, which is essentially a summing-up of the covenant, Moses emphasises the crucial requirement: 'You shall *hear*, O Israel, and you shall take care to act accordingly.' There can be no understanding, certainly no loving, without first hearing the words of God: God's promise, and his actions, must be pondered on unremittingly so that they begin to permeate every facet of life, the home, the family, the wider community. Already in the Old Testament the words spoken by God are becoming an integral part of human experience.

For Jews and Christians alike liturgical celebration today is far more than remembering the key events of this relationship: it is in actuality a reliving of the experience. In the Passover supper eaten each year, the events of the Exodus are actually re-experienced, and similarly the Easter Vigil in the Roman Easter rite is a reliving which begins with a fire outside the church building from which participants light candles and physically re-enact the exodus journey from darkness and enter into resurrection and light. Even today the actual words from Deuteronomy above are sealed in a container on the doors of many Jewish homes, but whether the injunction in the Bible to do this is obeyed literally or metaphorically the sentiment is the same: the people's part of the bargain is to keep God permanently in mind. Not for a minute or two before going to bed, not for an hour or so on Sunday, but as an inalienable part of daily life.

> *With your children and your wives (and the stranger too who is in your camp, whether he cuts wood or draws water for you), you are about to enter into the covenant of the Lord your God, a covenant ratified with dire sanctions, which he has made with you today, and by which, today, he makes a nation of you and he himself becomes a God to you, as he has promised and as he has sworn to your fathers Abraham, Isaac and Jacob. Not with you alone do I make this covenant today and pronounce these sanctions.*

> DEUTERONOMY 29: 11–14

THE PROMISED LAND

O God, listen to my prayer,
do not hide from my pleading,
attend to me and reply.
With my cares I cannot rest.
Oh that I had wings like a dove
to fly away and be at rest.
So I would escape far away
and take refuge in the desert.
I would hasten to find
a shelter from the raging wind,
from the destructive storm.
As for me I will cry to God
and the Lord will save me.

PSALMS 54/55: 2–3, 7–9, 17

One cannot help being struck by how frequently the theme of longing or desire recurs in the Scriptures. There are some religions that are centred on the elimination of desire (such as Buddhism): the Bible on the other hand points to all human desire – albeit sometimes misguided or unruly – as being the driving force of man's endless quest for God, who alone can fulfil it.

In particular we constantly find the longing for peace. 'Oh that I had wings like a dove to fly away and be at rest . . .' cries the psalmist. I am quite sure that peace is the most deep-rooted of all human desires, not the passive kind of peace that is simply the absence of anxiety or discord, but rather that much deeper peace which represents the achievement of a goal, the fullness of life. Peace is the destination which awaits us at the end of our journey. For the people of the Exodus it was represented by the promised land 'flowing with milk and honey', where there were no more enemies to be overcome and where they could live at peace and feel satisfaction in fulfilment of all human longing.

For them the progress to the promised land was beset by enemies. At times the mere sight of the threatening armies in their path must have made slavery in Egypt positively attractive, and the destination that was to be their inheritance must have seemed an awfully long way off. They were testing times, and when the people were fearful it was because they still did not understand that the promise 'I am with you' meant just that.

In our own journey towards peace we too will have to confront the powerful enemies of peace, and the desire that inspires us can become distorted; like the people of Israel we can be frightened into retreat by adversities we just can't tackle on our own. Some may be more potent than others, but they all have the same effect – dependence on drugs or alcohol, psychological or sexual problems, obsessions with money or power. All these are symptoms of our unfulfilled human longing. The aching void in our lack of peace can by our own efforts only be filled by counterfeit comforts. The obstacles may even be subconscious: bitterness, hidden resentments that my parents didn't bring me up properly, or that I've never been given the chances others have had, or even against God himself for not making me perfect! St John of the Cross commented that a bird could be tied to a tree by a heavy rope or by an invisible thread, but either way it could never fly away and be at rest.

On our own we are all bound, by various ropes and threads, but if we acknowledge that God has his desire too – a longing to lead his people to the promised land of peace and rest – then we shall discover in the simple words of the psalmist, a shepherd who will lead his flock beside tranquil water to revive them and give them rest. Note that these great promises of God which have come to us and been kept alive by the people of God beginning in Israel are for *all* peoples everywhere on earth. In Israel they still have today an ancient handwritten scroll of the Book of Isaiah, one of the great works of the literature of the Bible and in which the great promise of peace below is most beautifully and profoundly communicated.

> *On this mountain he will remove*
> *the mourning veil covering all peoples,*
> *and the shroud enwrapping all nations,*
> *he will destroy Death for ever.*
> *The Lord your God will wipe away*
> *the tears from every cheek;*
> *he will take away his people's shame*
> *everywhere on earth,*
> *for he has said so.*
> *That day it will be said: See, this is our God*
> *in whom we hoped for salvation;*
> *Our God is the one in whom we hoped.*
> *We exult and we rejoice*
> *that he has saved us;*
> *for the hand of the Lord*
> *rests on this mountain.*

ISAIAH 25: 7–10

I AM WITH YOU

*I will remain with the sons of Israel and I will be
their God. And so they will know that it is I the Lord
their God who brought them out of the land of
Egypt to live among them, I the Lord their God.*

EXODUS 29: 45–6

The most important part of the whole of God's covenant
promise to his people is the assurance that he will be with
them, will live *among them*. This is not the God magnificently
manifested in peals of thunder and consuming fire on the
mountain-top: this is the human face of God present in the
unspectacular events of the daily round, and it is a very
significant transition.

We are told that on Mount Sinai the people reacted with fear
and trembling, begging Moses to mediate with God on their
behalf: mortals cannot cope with transcendent holiness face to
face. Nor, as it turned out, could they cope with the alternative
– an abstraction, utterly remote from their experience. While
Moses is away those forty days and nights in the presence of
God, they get restless. If God is nowhere to be found then a
golden calf, which can be seen and felt, will at least satisfy one
part of their needs, the need to have a tangible, touchable God.

If they had been a little more patient (and we all need to learn
from this) their problem was being resolved, even as they
melted down their earrings for the molten effigy. They were
being offered not an image but a promise, and through this
promise God would be closer to them than they could possibly
know. True, you can't see a promise, but God provides them

with a tangible symbol of it. They are to erect a tabernacle tent, a kind of mobile shrine, which will represent his presence and inside there will be certain objects to remind them of who God is.

The Ark of the Covenant which contains the written word of God is a reminder of the importance of attentive listening to God's words. There is also a Throne of Mercy which represents God's forgiveness and enables men to understand what unconditional love is. Lighted candles signify God's life-giving light; a table with loaves of bread represents the family of God seated at a table and sharing consecrated bread. All of them symbols taken from everyday experience. The people are invited to acknowledge the presence of God among them by entering this sanctuary where, through the human faculties of hearing, seeing and feeling, they will receive a deeper spiritual understanding of who God is.

This is prayer. Israel's part of the covenant is to set itself apart to remain close to God, to understand who he is by experiencing his presence among them, and then to impart that knowledge to other nations. 'All the nations of the earth will be blessed by you.' As the history of this relationship unfolds, tabernacle becomes temple, temple becomes church (the Greek word for church is *ekklesia*, meaning set apart). The true Church is a people set apart for relationship – for prayer. From age to age God gathers a people who will set time 'apart', given to God in relationship, but specifically so that through them others will receive his blessings.

In the Gospels the people of God are referred to as stewards, the salt of the earth, the leaven in the dough. St Paul uses the description 'ambassadors', and I especially like the simile of St Francis of Assisi who prayed that God would make him a 'channel'. But the mainspring of all this is God dwelling *in* and *among* his people. In the Old Testament the incarnation is already beginning: the infinite already dwells within the confines of the earth.

Humour is not just an alleviation of pain, it also brings the infinite down to earth. God has no human form in Jewish theology, but he reveals a very human psyche in Jewish jokes. There he enters into the suffering and paradoxes of the world, and experiences the human condition. There he is immanent, if not incarnate, and a gossamer bridge of laughter stretches over the world, linking creatures of flesh and blood to the endlessness of the eternal and the paralysing power of the Lord of Hosts.

RABBI LIONEL BLUE: *Day Trips to Eternity*

CHAPTER FIVE

For Judgment Read Mercy

FAILURE AND FORGIVENESS

The Old Testament encourages people suffering from misfortune, weighed down by sin, to beg for mercy. It helps them to count on it; it reminds them of God's mercy in times of failure and when they have lost their trust in him. The Old Testament gives thanks and praise every time mercy shows itself in the life of an individual. In this way mercy is in contrast with justice and more profound.

JOHN PAUL II: *On God's Mercy*
(Shortened Version)

The Old Testament is indeed a striking witness to God's mercy. Mercy is a word with a rather old-fashioned ring to it nowadays, and has always suffered from being a somewhat inadequate translation of the original Hebrew. In due course we shall examine the concept more closely, but here we can take up one strand of its meaning, which is forgiveness.

In spite of the people's dismal failure at Mount Sinai – their resort to manufacturing a golden calf – God declares himself 'merciful and gracious, slow to anger and abounding in stead-fast love and faithfulness' (Exodus 34: 6). As the history of Israel develops we continue to find yet more apostasy: the people seem perpetually bent on 'playing the harlot', worshipping other gods and breaking their own commitment to a loving relationship with God.

As you might expect from Old Testament writers, whose primitive view of justice was that old adage of an eye for an eye and a tooth for a tooth, in those days the punishment should

[91]

always fit the crime, and there are some very colourful descriptions of God's exasperation, as well as his 'fiery anger'. But time and again it is his love that prevails and overcomes anger. The exasperation is at the stubborn refusal of his creation, whose raison d'être is for friendship and shared existence, to hear and understand him. He alone can provide this fulfilment, he was and still is utterly powerless before those who refuse his friendship. Love cannot manipulate, it can only permit freedom and that freedom can in turn result in the opposite, namely the violation of that relationship.

What we need to understand and distinguish is that there are *consequences* to this refusal of God's friendship, this self-assertion of independence of him, but it is quite wrong to view these consequences as punishment. If we examine what the relationship with God promises, we find light and love, intimacy, peace, joy and forgiveness; the consequences of rejection are their opposites, darkness and lovelessness, loneliness, confusion, bitterness and guilt. Instead of accepting and enjoying the former, we put up with the latter and, maybe, even come to believe that these are the norm.

In the biblical narratives Israel lurches from one disaster to another, but mercy remains the unremitting message of hope. The unconditional love promised in the covenant does not alter one jot, however unfaithful the people are. It is only human justice that requires punishment, and debts to be paid. Love cancels the debt. There is always a way back to love, to the father's heart, and his forgiveness does not condemn, but instead heals and restores dignity.

The words below are attributed to one of Israel's famous sons, David. A proven adulterer and a confessed murderer, no one understood human failure and weakness better than he. But he also understood God's forgiveness, saying at the end of his life that he would rather entrust himself to God's mercy than into the hands of men.

The Lord is compassion and love,
slow to anger and rich in mercy.
His wrath will come to an end.
He will not be angry for ever.
He does not treat us according to our sins,
nor repay us according to our faults.

PSALM 102/103: 8–10

THE MEANING OF MERCY

You see, Fyn, people can only love outside and can only kiss outside, but Mister God can love you right inside, and Mister God can kiss you right inside, so it's different. Mister God ain't like us; we are a little bit like Mister God but not much yet ... You see, Fyn, Mister God is different from us because he can finish things and we can't. I can't finish loving you because I shall be dead millions of years before I can finish, but Mister God can finish loving you, and so it's not the same kind of love, is it?

Mister God, This is Anna

In her five-year-old fashion Anna has got to the heart of what God's mercy involves. The word itself, mercy, does not have much currency nowadays and I suspect the reason for this is that it is such an inadequate translation of the original Hebrew, which has no fewer than four separate strands of meaning: (1) leaning over and reaching out to someone, (2) suffering with and sparing out of pity, (3) being soft, providing comfort like a mother, and (4) relieving someone, stopping their groans by helping them to breathe. The sheer richness of the biblical word offers enormous scope for reflection because it speaks volumes about the nature of God, even if we can only catch shades of the true meaning.

The first interpretation is the underlying message of God to man: 'I am with you'. The second and third illuminate the original meaning of the word compassion, to suffer *with* someone as echoed in Isaiah's famous passage: 'Ours were the sufferings he bore, ours the sorrows he carried' and indeed elsewhere in the same book 'As a mother comforts her child, so I will comfort you, my people'. The final interpretation is illustrated in the Book of Wisdom which describes God as the lover of life, keeping vigil, all the time helping us to breathe that breath of life he longs to give us. In short, mercy goes way beyond the particular ideas of forgiveness or compassion: it represents an all-encompassing love for each and every one of his creatures, which not only embraces human life but somehow enters into and shares its struggle.

One of the most vivid pictures of what I believe God's mercy to be came in a television programme I chanced to see not very long ago: it was about the treatment of autistic children at a special clinic in Hungary. Autistic children are, in a sense, isolated from society, their brains incapable of transmitting the necessary signals either for communication or movement. In Britain there is no special treatment that is effective: they are, as one parent described it, thrown onto the scrap-heap of life. Yet in the Hungarian clinic they refuse to give up hope and, in so doing, have made great breakthroughs.

They have discovered that if a child is given one-to-one treatment round the clock, it *can* produce results. The therapy involves endless hours of side by side involvement by the teachers; sometimes it can take months even to produce one movement in a limb or a flicker of recognition. Given this time and attention some of the children can eventually walk and attend school, and hope and dignity have been introduced into their lives. Watching these dedicated teachers, their hope and patience, I saw some of God's mercy keeping close vigil at the side of every helpless creature struggling for light and life.

It seemed to me that through sin and the circumstances of our lives we are spiritually handicapped, even paralysed and unable to respond, yet mercy does not give up but goes on working day and night to elicit some response. Prayer and relationship with God melts the frozen spirit and awakens us to the warmth of love. As we become more spiritually conscious we gently encounter our handicap – our condition of unloving – and only when this happens can we then look into the face of mercy and admit, like Francis Thompson, the poet, that 'of all earth's clotted clay I am the dingiest clot' and know we are loved *even so*, then 'my mourning will be turned into dancing and my sorrow into joy'.

> *O Lord, I cried to you for help*
> *and you, my God, have healed me.*
> *To you, Lord, I cried, to my God*
> *I made my appeal.*
> *The Lord listened and had pity.*
> *The Lord came to my help.*
> *For me you have changed my mourning into dancing.*
> *You have removed my sackcloth and girded me with joy.*
> *So my soul sings psalms to you unceasingly.*
> *O Lord my God, I will thank you for ever.*

PSALM 29/30: 3, 9, 11–12

THE PROBLEM OF EVIL

If only there were evil people somewhere insidiously committing evil deeds, and it was necessary only to separate them from the rest of us and destroy them. But the line dividing good and evil cuts through the heart of every human being, and who is willing to destroy a piece of his own heart? . . . Socrates taught us know thyself.

ALEXANDER SOLZHENITSYN:
The Gulag Archipelago

I suppose one way of summing up the Old Testament is to view it as a failed love story: God continually drawing the people into a covenant relationship, the people continually failing to respond. Yet, paradoxically, one can detect throughout that there is an instinctive understanding that happiness can in fact only be found in the love of the one true God. The great prayerbook of Israel, the Book of Psalms, reveals this ambiguity of wanting yet not wanting God – and Psalm 50/51 perhaps more poignantly than any of them. Have mercy and pity on me because I seem to have been born with an incapacity for loving you ('a sinner was I conceived'). It's you and you alone that I offend by my lack of response. I see my problem ('my sin is always before me'). But you know all about the human heart, can you help my heart ('in the secret of my heart teach me wisdom')? Can you create a pure and loving heart in me?

This age-old ambivalence is expressed by St Paul as doing what I don't want to do, and not doing what I want to do. And the same sentiments have been expressed in countless different ways ever since: it was not just Israel's problem, but everyone's as we seek to find God.

The psalmist identifies this lack of response as being the 'evil' aspect of himself – the other side of Solzhenitsyn's dividing line of the heart. But the evil is present only to the degree that love is absent, evil being a void that can only be filled with the presence of love. When that presence penetrates the emptiness and gradually fills it, then what is evil is no more.

Can we identify this mysterious emptiness within the human heart? One word perhaps will suffice: *self*. It is I, myself, occupying the centre stage of the universe, with everything revolving around me. This total focus of attention on self begins with small children: 'That's mine!' 'No, it isn't. It's mine!' And it continues to be reflected on the largest scale, in the Gulf War, in Northern Ireland and Israel. 'That belongs to me, it is mine.' Nuclear weapons exist merely to make sure I protect what's mine.

God speaks the same word in the Old Testament and in the New, and that word is love. Love shifts the focus away from self to God, and then from God to other people. But what Psalm 50 is saying is, *I* can't do it, I *can't* love you. Will *you* save me from my self-centredness and teach me to love? One of the signs of authentic prayer in a person is how unself-focused they are. Yet the trouble is, as we read in the Book of Jeremiah, the heart is more devious than anything. Only God can pierce its secrets and know whether in the heart of that kind, loving, generous person it is really 'number one' that rules within. Selfishness can be scrupulously hidden away – even from ourselves – especially under the guise of religion or good works or even personal charm.

The lesson that Solzhenitsyn learned through the circumstances of his arrest, imprisonment and exile is the lesson for us all: know yourself, know your own potential for evil, know the power of self-centredness. True, it takes courage to confront what is most unpalatable, but once understood it is a most blessed thing. For only then can we understand our need of God, our need of rescue, our need of love, which is our only means of overcoming evil.

Indeed you love truth in the heart.
Then in the secret of my heart
teach me wisdom.
O purify me then I shall be clean.
O wash me, I shall be whiter than
    snow.
A pure heart create for me, O God.
Put a steadfast spirit within me.
Do not cast me away from your presence
nor deprive me of your Holy Spirit.

PSALM 50/51: 8–9, 12–13

SIN

It often seems to me that what, from the outside,
seems to us sin and wickedness – violence, crime,
drug-taking, sexual promiscuity – is not so in God's
sight. Is it any more I wonder than the frantic
screaming of a child in the frightening darkness of
the night?
   An infant crying in the night:
   an infant crying for the light:
   and with no language but a cry. In Memoriam.

RUTH BURROWS: *To Believe in Jesus*

The Church and society can be – indeed they are – very specific about what is right and wrong, and the Bible itself provides clear guidelines. But notwithstanding the certainties and denunciations of the hell-fire preachers, no one can be specific about individual sin. Sin originates, the Scriptures point out, in the human heart, and no one apart from God can know what is in a person's heart; no one can determine from the outside what an inner motive is, nor weigh up all the circumstances involved. The all-too-frequent interpretation of Deuteronomy that 'the sins of the fathers are visited upon the children from generation to generation' implies some kind of inevitable divine punishment. But equally (and much more helpfully) it could be interpreted as an explanation of how people's weaknesses, selfishness and psychological disorders are handed down, to be passively absorbed and imitated.

What I think we *can* say is that sin, in its extreme form, is a total rejection of God who is love; it is a refusal even to contemplate a relationship where I am exposed to this love.

There again, such a rejection has to be understood at 'heart level'. I can be an atheist in an explicit way (for any number of reasons – perhaps because I've never been exposed to any authentic communication of who God is), yet implicitly, in my heart, I *do* respond to the dictates of conscience. I can be in love with nature, be a person of peace, joy and celebration – all of which are signs of God's loving presence in the heart of a person. On the other hand I can be explicitly Christian, deeply religious even, and yet at heart still reject God's truth.

It is my personal belief that God is closer to us than we are to ourselves. Though the sinner is insensitive to this presence, it is there nonetheless: the further someone is from wanting a relationship with God, the blinder they are to the possibility of realising it. As St Augustine concluded, when he looked back on his degenerate youth, God was within him all the time and it was he who was on the outside, so to speak. I remember a priest, who had himself suffered considerably in his life (and perhaps as a result had a particular gift in the ministry of confession), observing that he felt a tremendous sense of God's love enfolding each person at the very moment of their sinful act, no matter how seriously it might be viewed by the Church, society or anyone else.

Sin is wrong because of its consequences. The man or woman who walks out of a family commitment, for instance, leaves a trail of suffering that can cause damage which lasts years for those involved. But passing judgment does not soften that suffering one iota. Maybe what is more important is the context of sin: if I have a close relationship with someone where gradually love and mutual trust is built up, then I will be bonded to that person in such a way that betrayal becomes impossible. It won't be virtuous to keep true to the relationship, simply natural. This is what God asks of each of us, that we enter a relationship of trust in which we quite naturally grow in faithfulness. This is why the Church emphasises God's involvement in marriage. If a couple are growing in relationship to him, they will also be maturing in the art of unselfish loving. It is only pure unselfish love that can sustain a partnership for a lifetime.

The wages of sin is death, say the gloomy placards outside churches. But death here does not mean eternal punishment, it means what is anti-life. The effects of sin are negative, uncreative and destructive. What the human heart is crying out for in its sin is that real life-giving love which alone can save us from death and lead us to life.

> *The very fact that, despite his sin, the sinner continues to live shows that sin is always encompassed by an ever greater love which, precisely by accepting and justifying the sinner, exposes and overcomes the vanity of evil. An answer to the problems of evil and suffering becomes visible here in the mode of hope: precisely because it takes both sinful man and suffering seriously, it redeems sin and suffering by an even greater love. The hope is hope in the coming of absolute love that identifies itself with suffering and with the sufferer in the world. For sufferers the quest for God is a quest for divine compassion in the proper sense of this word, an identification of God with the suffering and death of human beings.*

> WALTER KASPER: *The God of Jesus Christ*

WHY DO WE SUFFER?

The question of God and the question of suffering belong together. We would not be able to suffer from our situation unless we had at least an implicit pre-apprehension of an undamaged, happy, fulfilled kind of existence, unless we were at least implicitly looking for salvation and redemption. Only because we as human beings are meant for salvation do we suffer our disastrous situation and rebel against it.

WALTER KASPER: *The God of Jesus Christ*

Suffering, in essence, is a signpost to God. It is a state we are all aware of, and most familiar with, where human effort, energy and ingenuity fall short. It is the point where we can be reduced to helplessness, and the burden can sometimes become too heavy for us to do anything but try to switch off the pain.

But how can all this point to God? It points to God because in suffering we can define the limitations of human life, but at the same time see the potential of what it is actually *meant* to encompass. In demonstrating that all is not well with the human race, it illuminates the possibility of moving beyond suffering to be saved and set free from it.

For instance I do not suffer in any way from not being able to fly: the impossibility of soaring up into the air like a bird causes me no anxiety. On the other hand I do suffer from not being able to heal sick friends or prevent famine; from failed relationships or insecurity; from the threat of nuclear warheads and the catastrophes flashed nightly onto the television screen. There, in a literal sense, I could switch off the pain by turning a knob, but in blotting out the reality might I not be switching off also the hope of redemption from it?

As we see so often, the Bible illustrates the point. The prodigal son, far from home and sharing the pigs' fodder, realises how much worse off he was than even one of his father's hired hands at home. He suffers, but if he had never left home, would he ever have appreciated what a father's love really meant? Perhaps sin and the effects of sin have to be experienced if we are to understand authentic love. Perhaps we need to experience the terrible consequences of love's absence before we can cry out in our own personal dark night 'may your kingdom come!' with real heartfelt conviction. As exiles in a strange land 'mourning and weeping in a vale of tears' we can focus our hearts more clearly on the peace and joy of home 'where every tear will be wiped away and there will be no more mourning and sadness' (Revelation 21:4).

In his book on the problem of pain C. S. Lewis wrote that pain was the only opportunity for the sinner to amend: 'until the evil man finds evil unmistakably present in his existence in the form of pain, he is enclosed in an illusion'. His analogy of pain is that it is a megaphone that arouses the deaf world.

The most positive and hopeful aspect of suffering is its power to unite people, to invoke that compassion with the suffering of others which is a reflection of God's own mercy. No one knows who wrote the words printed below, but they were found on a piece of wrapping paper near the body of a dead child at Ravensbruck, the concentration camp where 92,000 people lost their lives. They show love can be borne in the midst of appalling suffering. Even more, they show how if we want a tangible vision of who God is, we need look no further than at the 'greatness of heart' in the people who know him.

> *O Lord, remember not only the men and women of goodwill, but also those of ill-will. But do not remember all the suffering they have inflicted on us; remember the fruits we have bought thanks to this suffering – our comradeship, our loyalty, our humil-*

ity, our courage, our generosity, the greatness of heart which has grown out of all this, and when they come to the judgment let all the fruits we have borne be their forgiveness.

ANON

A NEW COVENANT

Joy has vanished from our hearts;
* our dancing has been turned to mourning.*
The garland has fallen from our heads.
* Woe to us, because we have sinned! . . .*
But you, Lord God, you remain for ever . . .
* You cannot mean to abandon us for good?*
Make us come back to you, Lord God, and we
* will come back.*

LAMENTATIONS 5: 15–16, 19, 20–1

The one thing that redeems Israel's chequered relationship with God, with its weaknesses, breakdowns and inability to respond to the covenant, is the inherited perception that God's promise remains in spite of their failures. In succeeding generations there is always a small number of people – 'a faithful remnant' – who manage to understand and hold to this promise. They are what we referred to earlier as the 'sources close to', the people of prayer whose underlying message does not waver: return to the covenant relationship.

These prophetic voices are, not unnaturally, the most persuasive at times of national defeat and exile – which the people take to be some form of punishment. But their true exile is to have wandered off, as it were, from God's loving relationship, and the prayer above reflects this realisation. It contains a very significant plea: *make us* return to you, indicating that they have at last arrived at the point of understanding their human frailty and, more importantly, their inability to reciprocate God's love. This self-knowledge is a landmark on the spiritual journey, a milestone and one never easily reached.

What God promises through the prophets is that he *will* answer their need and their inability to respond. He will do something new. He will initiate a covenant in the hearts of his people. The prophets proclaim it again and again. 'I shall give you a new heart, and put a new spirit in you; I shall remove the heart of stone from your bodies and give you a heart of flesh instead. I shall put my spirit in you and make you keep my laws' (Ezekiel 36:26). There's the answer to the prayer at the beginning, quite unequivocal. Then Jeremiah: 'Deep within them I will plant my law, writing it on their hearts. There will be no need for neighbour to teach neighbour, or brother to teach brother . . . No, they will all know me' (Jeremiah 31:33). God is somehow going to reveal himself and teach us love at the deepest heart level.

The prophets' message is one of waiting and hoping – the same Hebrew word conveys both meanings. Israel is invited to live in a state of hope that awaits God's certain mercy, and that is the same condition of the journey of prayer: waiting, hoping for what the Scriptures call 'things beyond the mind of man, all that God has prepared for those who love him' (1 Corinthians 2: 9). Prayer, if it's authentic, will always gently reveal our lack of unselfish loving, and at the same time teach us to wait and hope for God to do something new in us, something only he can initiate.

> No need to recall the past,
> no need to think about what was done before.
> See, I am doing a new deed,
> even now it comes to light; can you not see it?
> Yes, I am making a road in the wilderness,
> paths in the wilds.
>
> ISAIAH 43: 18–19

I WILL COME

Oh, that you would tear the heavens open
and come down
—at your Presence the mountains would melt,
as fire sets brushwood alight,
as fire causes water to boil —
to make known your name to your enemies,
and make the nations tremble at your Presence,
working unexpected miracles
such as no one has ever heard of before.

ISAIAH 64: 1–3

It is still, even today, a trait of human nature to equate God's approval with material achievement and success (and, just as wrong, to interpret pain and suffering as a sign of God's disfavour: 'What have I done to deserve this?'). Israel, demoralised and defeated, hears through its prophets that God is going to do something new, that he is going to come to them. Their reaction, as described in the prayer above, is to invoke him as some kind of avenging fire that will demonstrate to their enemies precisely what God's favour to a nation means. And in truth, when we observe the wars that are still waged in his name, the 'I'll show them' mentality hasn't changed much. The God who yearns for love is so often sought for other motives.

It is the prophecies of Isaiah, throbbing with expectancy, that give us the sharpest focus in the Old Testament to the promise of God-with-us. 'Courage, do not be afraid. Look, your God is coming; he is coming to save you' (Isaiah 35: 4). On one level they do invite interpretation of future triumphs and domination, pointing to a saviour and deliverer, a royal king through the line of David. God will 'tear the heavens open', but

[108]

not in the way Israel anticipates. To continue with Isaiah: 'there is a child born to us, a son given to us and dominion is laid upon his shoulders' – but the son will be Prince of Peace, and his dominion 'a peace that has no end' (Isaiah 9: 6).

Although this messiah king will have power, he is also presented as a servant of the people, who will bring good news to the poor and bind up broken hearts. He will bring freedom to the oppressed, comfort to the suffering, joy to those in sorrow. But there is an even greater significance to this revolutionary servant king: he will be *born* for us. That is the ultimate meaning of 'mercy', its culminating expression. God, this 'mighty God', will enter into the human condition and there will be no human experience he will not share. He will go all the way *with us* even to death itself. In the context of Israel's plight this must have seemed a paradox, even something of a let-down; but Isaiah is quite clear about it. The servant king will die, to overcome death.

To reflect on why this should be necessary, we should perhaps pose a question. How *can* I comprehend God as love and the idea of that love as a shared experience? I can hear the words of love, but can I understand what they mean without seeing love in action? Certainly not at a distance, with a God metaphorically on the mountain-top and me rooted to the earth. Like an autistic child I need a God working one-to-one with me, to show me what love is. This can only happen if God condescends to reach me where I am.

> Sing, rejoice,
> daughter of Zion;
> for I am coming
> to dwell in the middle of you
> – it is the Lord who speaks.
> Many nations will join the Lord
> on that day;
> they will become his people . . .
> Let all mankind be silent before the Lord,
> for he is awaking and is coming from his holy
> dwelling.
>
> ZECHARIAH 2: 14–15, 17

CHAPTER SIX

The Human Face of God

INCARNATION

All that came to be had life in him and that life was the light of men, a light that shines in the dark, a light that darkness could not overpower. The Word was the true light that enlightens all men; and he was coming into the world. He was in the world that had its being through him, and the world did not know him. He came to his own domain and his own people did not accept him. But to all who did accept him he gave power to become children of God, to all who believe in the name of him who was born not out of human stock or urge of the flesh or will of man but of God himself.

JOHN 1: 4–5, 9–13

What the creation narrative in Genesis shows, if nothing else, is the story of a development, a process of creation culminating in Man. Scientists may take issue with the order in which the various life forms appeared, but not with the essential message that man 'inherited' an earth in which seas and continents were formed, and in which fish and birds, reptiles and mammals existed. Today, with rather more information at our disposal, we can understand more about the natural evolutionary process: the awakening of life, its gradual development and growth, and its constant adaptation to change. And we can recognise that there were critical points in man's physical development – perhaps when one day a four-footed creature first stood up and nothing was ever the same again.

The Bible is also the record of another evolution, man's spiritual evolution, which follows the same on-going pattern of awakening, growth and adaptation. St Paul describes it as

A Journey into God

humanity groping and feeling its way towards God (Acts 17). It is, if you like, a parallel to the almost imperceptible retreat of the ice ages which ultimately liberated man's physical development: the unfreezing of man's spirit until it melts into the realisation and acceptance of God's purpose for creation.

The incarnation represents the critical, decisive, point in this spiritual evolution, when God breaks into history to demonstrate that the growth of the spirit is not separate from life but integral to it. We have briefly traced in this book the history of God's offer and the seeming helplessness of the sinful human heart to respond – an evolutionary impasse, which only God's mercy in its fullest flowering can remove. Thus God himself enters into the human condition (*in carne*) in flesh and for the first time in history a man, Jesus, actually fully accepts God's offer. A 'new creation' dawns, and nothing will be the same again.

The essence of evolution is that it is a progression; nothing is fixed or static. The process continues and the way ahead lies in our own personal spiritual evolution. As St John explains we now all have 'the power' to become children of God. In the life and teaching of Jesus we *learn* how to become a child of God and receive his gift of eternal life, which he has universally accepted on our behalf: what he received from the Father, we receive from him. The life that enlightens *all* men.

> *The father uttered one word;*
> *that word is his Son,*
> *and he utters him for ever in everlasting silence;*
> *and in silence the soul has to hear it.*

ST JOHN OF THE CROSS

AS MEN ARE

His state was divine,
yet he did not cling
to his equality with God
but emptied himself to assume the condition of a slave
and became as men are . . .

PHILIPPIANS 2: 6–7

There are plenty of people who can happily accept that Jesus existed as a man, but who have problems coming to terms with his divinity at the same time. Equally, I suspect, there are many others who accept 'his state was divine' yet find it hard to grasp the reality of his humanity: somehow being the Son of God precluded any genuine claim to be human as well. Looking back, I realise that my own belief on the subject was just as ambiguous, confined to vague notions that he was a kind of heavenly envoy, a God-dressed-up-as-man figure whose role was really rather mysterious.

What profoundly changed my attitude was one particular moment of realisation some years ago. At the time I belonged to a readers' group at our local church, which involved spending time preparing the readings for the forthcoming Sunday. We were asked to take a particular passage, spend thirty minutes or so reflecting on its meaning and then share our thoughts with the rest of the group. One day on a train journey to London I looked at the passage I'd been given: it was Mark's account of the events in the Garden of Gethsemane before Jesus' arrest.

In all honesty, although I had been a Christian for several years, that was the first time I had ever reflected deeply on a passage of Scripture. The obvious truth of what I was reading struck me like a bolt: Jesus was *truly* a man, totally like us in every sense. Here was real fear and anxiety, and the humiliation of discovering the depths of human helplessness. The spirit is willing but the flesh is weak. In that one phrase is all the despair of mortality, and yet this is God speaking, God experiencing human limitations not from afar but right here where we are. 'A man like us in all things', a man who knows what it is to be betrayed by a loved one, who knows the loneliness of having no one around at the crucial moment, who begs not to have to face death!

I suppose we all have recourse from time to time to one of the false gods we encountered earlier: perhaps before this mine had been the god who 'waits for us to make mistakes'. But now I had discovered the real God by discovering the real Jesus, the man who understands human frailty from within. The compassionate God is one who suffers with us in our weaknesses and failures, and in Jesus we have mercy and compassion personified. The first vital lesson *we* have to learn from *him* is how to be human and live happily within the framework of our inadequacies.

The great theologian Karl Rahner has described human beings as being created by God with an emptiness, a space which only God can fill. Is it not incredible that the God who created that space should become empty himself, share our emptiness, in order that he can show us how it can be fulfilled?

> *During his life on earth he offered up prayer and entreaty, aloud and in silent tears, to the one who had the power to save him out of death, and he submitted so humbly that his prayer was heard. Although he was Son, he learnt to obey through suffering, but having been made perfect, he became for all who obey him the source of eternal salvation.*

> HEBREWS 5: 7–9

[116]

THE LIFE OF JESUS

It is written in the prophets:
They will all be taught by God,
and to hear the teaching of the Father,
and learn from it,
is to come to me.

JOHN 6: 45

I once had to attempt to say something about God to a large, rather uninterested group of sixth-formers. I asked them to raise their hand if any of them would like to hear God actually speaking directly to them. It seemed from where I was sitting that no one in fact refrained from raising their hand. I imagine this would be the reaction in most cases, for however cynical or unbelieving we may be, the prospect of a one-to-one encounter with God would be too interesting to turn down.

What the Gospels teach us, and what the whole journey of prayer reveals to us, is that this is precisely what we *can* have. God's incarnate programme for the world was not a thirty-three-year fixture in history, but an on-going event; not a fleeting visit to earth, but a perpetual presence through all those who bear the name Christian, and indeed all those who implicitly respond to light and truth.

The passage from St John at the beginning encapsulates the very meaning of discipleship: following, hearing, learning and applying what I learn in my own life. In this way I become Christ-ianised. Christ in Greek means anointed: as I watch and listen, I learn how I too can become God's 'anointed one'. In the gospel accounts we are able to hear what Jesus said and watch what Jesus did. His life, though physically circumscribed by history, lives on through those who respond as disciples. 'He who sees me, sees the Father,' Jesus tells us. 'My words are not my words but the words of the Father who sent me.' God *is* speaking directly to us, today as he was then.

One reading of St John's famous prologue is that, in the life of Jesus, the word *started* to become flesh and that it will take a whole world responding to him to complete the incarnation. Some hope, one might say, looking at a world torn and twisted, largely deaf to Jesus' message from God of the love that can fill the emptiness and eventually unite creation.

And yet, we are occasionally granted the faintest glimpses of what the incarnation ultimately means. One of the most tangible visions, if you like, of hope for the future struck me on the day of the Live Aid concert in 1985. With the God-given gift of high technology and satellite television – not to mention the glorious sunshine – it was suddenly possible to have a perception of the world as a community of love (and not least among the young). For one day nations were united in the fight against famine. It wasn't the money raised that was so impressive, but the few precious moments of universal communion in one common purpose, with no motivation other than goodness and generosity. There were tears for a suffering world, yes, but also joy and celebration in sharing a hope for the future.

When the incarnation, like leaven in the dough, has worked its way all through the human race, the global village or world community will no longer be a dream but a reality. When love reigns there will be no more famine, 'no more mourning, no more sadness. The world of the past has gone' (Revelation 21: 4).

Father, Righteous One,
the world has not known you,
but I have known you,
and these have known
that you have sent me.
I have made your name known to them

and will continue to make it known,
so that the love with which you loved me may be in them,
and so that I may be in them.

JOHN 17:25–6

THE DEATH OF JESUS

Unless a wheat grain falls to the ground and dies,
it remains a single grain;
but if it dies
it yields a rich harvest.

JOHN 12: 24

What the death of Jesus on the cross reveals most powerfully is the 'humanity' of God, and what it means to be human. That is to say God is not only identifying totally with us: he is revealing our own identity to us. Of the many and profound implications of the crucifixion, this simple truth stands out – yet it is one that for the most part is evaded.

Mankind (as we have already reflected) is created for a glory beyond its imagination, but the work of creation is not yet finished: we are not fulfilled, not yet complete. Yet for most of us our lives are spent denying this fact. We rail and struggle against our human limitations, but we cannot really deny they exist, the mistakes and weaknesses and disappointments, the powerlessness in the face of problems. So much of our life is wasted by trying to deny our vulnerability: perhaps we refuse ever to be wrong about anything, perhaps we convince ourselves our failures are the fault of others, of our parents, or our job, or our marriage. Sometimes, even, the pressures of our own cover-up of our limitations are what bring on stress, depression or disease. We are, in short, striving to be super-human or like gods ourselves.

God takes on human flesh to reconcile us to our vulnerability: he did not deny it, nor should we. It means relinquishing any power I might have to manipulate circumstances, surrendering to being a failure in the eyes of others, accepting weakness, not pretending to have all the answers. Of course it's quite incomprehensible, such utter vulnerability. In human terms it is a scandal and a folly, and is there any one of us who would not instinctively draw his sword, like Peter, and refuse to accept the humiliation of it?

Yet that is the momentous truth of covenant love: that God himself is willing to surrender to his creatures, and demonstrate a love that hands itself over completely to others regardless of the consequences. No one says it's easy. Jesus himself, having accepted the human lot, fought against his total surrender and cried out, we're told, 'in loud entreaties and silent tears' for the strength to say not what I want, but what you want.

To be emptied of all self, *that* is dying, a lifetime of learning how to surrender and letting myself metaphorically fall into the uncomprehending darkness of the earth like a grain of wheat, with nothing to offer or show or feel except a complete trust in God's promise – but with the example of Jesus always with us to prove to us that there *will* be a rich harvest.

> *Only prayer reveals the precipitous depths of our poverty. Submission to it involves an awareness of someone else. We are so poor that even our poverty is not our own: it belongs to the mystery of God. In prayer we drink the dregs of our poverty, professing the richness engendered of someone else: God. The ultimate word of impoverished man is 'Not I, but thou'.*
>
> JOHANNES METZ: *Poverty of Spirit*

THE RESURRECTION OF JESUS

The silkworms come from seeds about the size of grains of pepper. When the warm weather comes and the leaves appear on the mulberry tree, the seeds start to live, for they are dead till then. The worms nourish themselves on mulberry leaves until, having grown to full size, they settle on some twigs. There with their little mouths they go about spinning thick little cocoons in which they enclose themselves. The silkworm, which is very fat and ugly, then dies, and in a little while a butterfly which is very pretty comes forth from the cocoon.

ST TERESA OF AVILA

This is the parable that St Teresa used to try to explain to her spiritual daughters what happens when a soul gives its life over to God. The life of the silkworm becomes a metaphor for life, death and resurrection and what the journey into God involves. The silkworm – she is saying – gives its whole life to what seems to be a preparation for death. In reality, it is a preparation for life.

To follow through Teresa's analogy, what sustains, nourishes and gives strength is prayer – as we can observe in the life of Jesus. He is showing us how to prepare for resurrection, living in close relationship with his Father, conducting his life in such a way that he can set time apart to be in his presence, entrusting himself completely to him. At the same time he shows us that this does not mean being set apart from ordinary life or community: yielding totally to his Father, he yields totally to people.

[122]

All God asks of us is that we love, and love is the handing over of self to God *and* others. As we have observed, we are constantly appalled at our own inadequacies in this department, not to mention having to bear the pain of its absence in the world around us. But Teresa's silkworms are souls that have to *labour* in love, to weave that cocoon of death (to self), and part of this death is recognising our own poverty in loving. Jesus in the Garden saw so clearly how weak humanity is, but he also through his tears and prayers *received* the strength to say 'not what *I* want'.

On the cross we see the end of the story of a journey into God: self annihilated, life handed over. It is the very moment of resurrection, revealing for ever what love incarnate really is. What it isn't is flexing our muscles, gritting our teeth and saying I will love or else. It is being vulnerable, a willing spirit in a weak flesh calling on God for assistance. The work of spinning that cocoon of death of self-centredness can only be sustained by God leaning over and helping us. In prayer we present our worm-like ugliness – our unloving natures – to God and ask him to work the miracle of transformation. All prayer is about wanting that to happen, the worm longing to become a butterfly. But how can it happen? How can the life, death and resurrection of Jesus help me? To be continued, in the next reflection.

> *The formative power of Christ lies in the formlessness of the seed which dies and dissolves in the earth to rise again, not in its own form as seed but as an ear of corn. This rhythm, this descent into the earth with its humility and self-sacrifice, is characteristic of Christianity as a whole and of its fruitfulness . . . It must, like its founder, surrender itself completely and sacrifice its particular form – without the least dread of being let go and letting go of oneself. For if the world is to believe, it can only believe in Love.*
>
> H. U. VON BALTHASAR: *Love Alone*

HOLY SPIRIT, LORD AND GIVER OF LIFE

If Christ is in you then your spirit is life itself because you have been justified; and if the Spirit of him who raised Jesus from the dead is living in you, then he who raised Jesus from the dead will give life to your own mortal bodies through his Spirit living in you.

ROMANS 8: 10–11

Here I have to come clean! The first thing to be said about trying to communicate the nature of the Holy Spirit is that it can't be done. Faced with the central mystery of the Christian faith even the New Testament writers struggled with language and imagery, conscious that when we use the word 'spirit' we are venturing into unknown territory. And yet it is a word we use commonly enough with an adequate appreciation of its meaning. An independent sort of person might be a free spirit, or I might be feeling tired today but still in good spirit. We speak of the spirit of an age or even of an occasion. People who have lost close friends or relations can still often feel them near in spirit. Of course all these have different nuances, but all express our collective sense of an extra dimension above normal experience.

In short it is something we can 'understand' but not define. At best, like the biblical authors, we can resort to paraphrase. They talked of spirit as 'life' (indeed we still refer to a spirited person as full of life), and drew their illustrations of it from nature. Thus God's Spirit hovers over the earth, bringing forth a creation teeming with life. In the same way his Spirit is also a

[124]

wind, invisible and uncontainable, the very breath of life which God breathes into his creatures.

Another recurring image of the life-giving spirit is that of water, for where there is no water life cannot exist. Thus Ezekiel describing a river that flows from the temple where God's presence dwells: 'wherever the river flows all living creatures teeming in it will live, wherever the water goes it brings health and life. The trees on the river banks will bear fruit that never withers because this water comes from God' (Ezekiel 47). The other symbol of this life-force from God is fire: as gold is purified in a furnace, God's Spirit purifies the human heart rendering it capable of pure love. In his beautiful poem, 'The Living Flame of Love', St John of the Cross describes this flame as tenderly wounding the soul in its deepest centre.

When Jesus embarked on his public ministry he symbolically received the Holy Spirit by the baptism of water. As a man, that is to say, he allowed something to happen to him – if I can use an analogy of my own, he got 'connected' to the source of life. An appliance can only fulfil its function, only come to life as it were, if it is connected to the mains. The life that can animate *us*, spiritually, is divine. It is the Father's 'presence' within human existence, and at his baptism the Son received what we could perhaps call the first instalment of this divine life which enabled him to become the 'first of many brothers'.

Jesus the man lived but thirty-three years, but Christ the anointed one (as St Paul explains) lives on through the body of believers. The power-supply is permanently switched on: the Holy Spirit, which proceeds from the Father and the Son continues to work in the Church and the world ultimately to bring all creation to a new birth which leads to resurrection and eternal life.

All that is hidden, all that is plain, I have come to know,
instructed by Wisdom who designed them all . . .
She is a breath of the power of God,
pure emanation of the glory of the Almighty;

hence nothing impure can find a way into her.
She is a reflection of the eternal light,
untarnished mirror of God's active power,
image of his goodness.

WISDOM 7: 21, 25–6

LIFE, A JOURNEY INTO JOY

Then I saw a new heaven and a new earth; the first
heaven and the first earth had disappeared now, and
there was no longer any sea. I saw the holy city and
the new Jerusalem coming down from God out of
heaven, as beautiful as a bride all dressed for her
husband. Then I heard a loud voice call from the
throne: 'You see this city? Here God lives among
men. He will make his home among them; they shall
be his people and he will be their God; his name is
God-with-them. He will wipe away all tears from
their eyes; there will be no more death, and no more
mourning or sadness. The world of the past has
gone.'

REVELATION 21: 1–4

When Jesus promised us the gift of his spirit, he also promised
the gift of his risen life. 'I will not leave you orphans, I will
come back to you,' he promised. 'In a short while the world
will no longer see me but you will see me, because I live and you
will live' (John 14: 18–19). What the incarnation invites us to
participate in is resurrection *life*, to be men and women of
hope, to celebrate life – being alive. Jesus came, he tells us, that
we might have life to the full: his own imagery of heaven is that
of the banquet. When the world – like the prodigal son –
returns to the Father's house there will be one hell of a
celebration (or rather one heaven of a celebration!) because the
prodigal will have returned to life (Luke 15: 24).

There is a danger that Christianity can become exclusively
Crosstianity, where suffering and deprivation become ends in
themselves. The fight against poverty or famine of course must

go on unremittingly and the sharing of resources must be a priority, but precisely because we want everyone to be equally rich, not equally poor. The good things of life are just as much a part of God's creation, ultimately to be enjoyed by everyone.

Hope is the key to joy, and participation in resurrection life means believing, hoping and bearing all things. I believe in God's unconditional love for me in spite of my weaknesses and failures, because Jesus has revealed this. I hope in a future where God's reign *will* be established on earth, and I bear with the suffering that has to be endured but with my eyes fixed firmly on the future when pain and suffering will cease.

The alternative is to live locked in a protective shell which will shield me from pain – but which will equally shield me from real joy too. Those who cling to sorrow with no expectancy of moving beyond the present situation are only accepting half-life. I have a friend who is a marvellous example of someone who utterly refuses to cling to suffering. A rare disease effectively and suddenly deprived him of his sight, which could have meant total disaster if he'd *allowed* it to ruin his life. Instead, a younger man whom he had trained in his own skills became a partner, and together my friend's long experience and the other man's sight continued a creative career.

That is what resurrection LIFE is about: not being immune to pain, injustice, betrayals, helplessness, but not letting them dominate. Joy and celebration are as integral to human life as suffering and dying, and if we need only one good reason to embark on the journey of prayer, it is to enable God to teach us the way to be authentically happy.

> *I am no longer trying for perfection by my own efforts . . . I want only the perfection that comes through faith in Christ and is from God and based on faith . . . All I can say is that I forget the past and I strain ahead for what is still to come; I am racing for the finish for the prize to which God calls us upwards to receive in Christ Jesus . . . If there is some point on which you see things differently, God will*

*make it clear to you; meanwhile let us go forward on
the road that has brought us to where we are.*

PHILIPPIANS 3: 9, 13–15, 16

CHAPTER SEVEN

'I Matter'

THE WONDER OF ME

If I asked darkness to cover me
and light to become night around me,
that darkness would not be dark to you,
night would be as light as day.

It was you who created my inmost self,
and put me together in my mother's womb;
for all these mysteries I thank you:
for the wonder of myself,
for the wonder of your works.

PSALM 138/139: 11–14

Is there anyone, anywhere, who can honestly admit to the truth of their own wonder and beauty? If so, I imagine it is a rare phenomenon. And I am not thinking now of those of us who seem rather pleased with – even proud of – themselves on occasions: deep-seated egotism is most likely to be a symptom of a massive lack of self-acceptance, and a means of concealing it. I'm sure one of the commonest causes of dis-ease in people is this acute lack of self-acceptance on their deepest level. Beneath the role-playing we can so easily condemn ourselves to a lifetime of covering up what we think is the reality in order to present a credible exterior.

What we cannot hope to grasp, outside the context of a relationship with God in prayer, is that our worst fears about ourselves are utterly unfounded: our very fragility, for God, is our most profound potential for wonder and beauty since it was he who created us as we are. As Isaiah (29: 16) put it, the earthen pot is dependent on the potter, who shapes and fashions it according to the beauty of his secret design. 'Thus can the clay say to the potter, Fool?'

We can only assume that the psalmist quoted at the beginning has travelled a long way in the spiritual life, because he has understood the reality of his own creation. To hide from self-knowledge may seem the safest course, but how wrong it is. Perhaps we *can't* feel that we are beautiful, or even begin to appreciate the scale of this wonder, but we *do* need to open ourselves to the possibility of it, for as St Augustine maintained we begin to find God when we begin to find ourselves.

Maybe we can make a start to the process by contemplating our own uniqueness. From the moment of our births – the one event in our lives in which we are totally passive because we have no chance to either choose or not choose to be born – we are special. Now if you think about this unique event of the gift of your own life it is impossible to deny that quite objectively you are extremely special. No one who lives, or has ever lived, has a thumb-print quite like yours and we are now told by even more advanced science that a genetic print can identify any individual out of billions. The same can be said of faces, absolutely no one who has ever lived has a face quite like your face. There are TV impersonators or lookalikes, but they never actually look quite the same. We can say the same too of voices – there isn't a voice anywhere that is the same as your voice; every life is individual, like a rare and precious gem that cannot be matched, and every person whatever they may look like or feel like is infinitely beautiful in a way that no one else is. Each of us is extraordinary. The literal Hebrew translation of the psalm above is 'I thank you Lord that I am wonderful'. I offer this as a starting-point for consideration of the extract below. It is a most moving account of how someone came to acknowledge this uniqueness. It comes from the writings of a young American woman who, dying of cancer, kept a diary of all the consequent horrors and traumas from diagnosis to death. She was not a religious woman, but here are her conclusions.

> *Mystery, what a mystery this life is. The plants are filling out. The garden out back of our home sprouts*

one half-inch here, an inch there, and I am changing too; cancer plods on from node to node, remarkable and not remarkable at all, like summer itself. Just another growing season after all. Is this resignation? I hope not. I do not intend to give up without a struggle, but more and more I see myself as a thread in a huge and royal tapestry — important to the central design but having an end, a place, a physical destination. I think of the young daughter in Satyajit Ray's Panther Panchali, *spinning, whirling in the rain, her hair flying out like a flag the day she died. No one is special, are they, when all is said and done? And of course each of us is very special, very singular, carrying weight. I matter. I would like to open the window tonight and yell that outside. I* matter. *Or go down and lie next to the plants and whisper it.*

DOROTHEA LYNCH: *Exploding into Life*

THE WHY OF ME

Yes, you love all that exists, you hold nothing of what you
  have made in abhorrence,
for, had you hated anything, you would not have formed it.
And how, had you not willed it, could a thing persist,
how be conserved if not called forth by you?
You spare all things because all things are yours, Lord
  lover of life.

WISDOM 11: 25–7

I think it was Gandhi who said that if you want to find God, don't bother to look any further than the person next to you, and this is something I myself am convinced of. What the dying Dorothea (in our last reflection) came to understand so vividly was that she, *like everyone else*, is an indispensable component of God's huge composition and that her life was as vital as any other in its final completion.

Doubtless we can all think of one or two of our acquaintances whose indispensability seems highly unlikely, and not least ourselves. But these are distortions on the surface; the gold – perhaps as yet unrefined – lies underneath in every life. I recently heard a famous photographer interviewed on the radio. He had photographed top models, the rich and famous all over the world and his pictures were greatly admired. The interviewer put a question to him: 'What happens when you are commissioned to photograph someone ugly? What do you do to make them look beautiful?' Without a moment's hesitation he replied quite simply that there was no such thing as an ugly person. There was always beauty, without exception.

There was always, he went on, some other dimension to a person who might not be physically beautiful. Just as deaf people, for instance, are extra-sensitive to sound or touch, so he could always observe some particular sensitivity in physically plain people, and his skill as a photographer was to catch that with the camera.

When it comes to ourselves, we can often be our own cameras creating our own self-images. I may feel much more like St Paul's 'cracked earthen vessel' than a rare and exquisite Ming vase, but my feelings are not the true lens. I exist because God created me and wanted me absolutely as I am – and you absolutely as you are. Our birth is not optional: we exist because we are chosen. God, the lover of life, is imprinted on all of life and each thing in creation reflects something of his beauty, each in a different way.

The journey of prayer has to start off with this frame of mind, with this consideration of the why of my life. Why me? Because I am wanted. We are not approaching some distant God whom we have to find by our own efforts or track down like orienteers, but one who created each individual for himself as part of his plan. He wants us all as we are, not as we may think we are. I am not lightly underestimating how difficult this exercise might be. I once gave a retreat to a beautiful group of young people in their teens and early twenties – on asking them to consider what we've discussed above, quite a few were reduced to tears, quite unable to comprehend their own value and worth. The wretchedness of some people's harsh and painful experience distorts and hides this truth of our innate beauty, but in prayer we are gently coaxed out of our hiding.

> *Come then, my love,*
> *my lovely one, come.*
> *My dove, hiding in the clefts of the rock,*
> *in the coverts of the cliff,*
> *show me your face,*
> *let me hear your voice;*
> *for your voice is sweet*
> *and your face is beautiful.*

SONG OF SONGS 2: 13

I ONLY KNOW THAT I AM LONGING

O God, you are my God, for you I long.
For you my soul is thirsting, my body pines for you
like a dry weary land without water.

PSALM 62/63: 1

That inner self which we call the soul does not come as an optional extra: it is in fact the vital force that animates our entire existence. The soul is the true *Eros*, an arrow hurtling in only one direction – to God. We are familiar with the concept of Eros through the work and writings of Freud, but what he described as Eros represented only one strand of the whole of its meaning. Sexual desire is only one element of that latent dynamism that dictates our lives. There are many forms of desire – for beauty, for power, for wealth, for fame, for love – all of them tributaries of a powerful river that carries us along.

There are many descriptions of the symptoms of this hidden force. For St Augustine it was restlessness, echoing the psalmist's cry: 'You have made us for yourself, O God, and our hearts can find no rest until they rest in you.' We often describe someone as being 'full of life' when we might more accurately describe them as being 'full of Eros', a desire for more and more of life and more experiences. The restlessness exists because life is never quite enough. We can have money, success, perfect marriage, wonderful children, yet there co-exists a dissatisfaction that cannot be assuaged. Of course it can be sublimated while we occupy ourselves in creating ever-expanding horizons, but with tragic inevitability there will come a time when there are no new heights to scale, life is passing and what we thought would bring completeness hasn't. We are left only with that restless ache.

The Bible regularly communicates this restlessness as a thirsting for God. 'Like the deer that yearns for running streams so my soul is yearning for God' says the psalmist (41/42). When Jesus meets the woman by Jacob's Well he explains that the water which can quench her physical thirst cannot satisfy her spiritual thirst. 'Anyone who drinks the water that I shall give, will never be thirsty again' (John 4:14) he promises. Prayer is learning how to channel that deep thirst in the right direction.

Prayer begins with nothing other than a natural human longing, what St John of the Cross called 'woundedness', a wound in the deep centre of the soul that longs for love. Whether we know it or whether we acknowledge it or not, that restless striving is a longing for union with God. None of us is immune, and there are periods in our lives when we are more aware of this nameless longing than at others. Adolescence is certainly one, and the following extract from *The Diary of Anne Frank* describes it most poignantly.

> *The sun is shining, the sky is deep blue, there is a lovely breeze and I'm longing – so longing – for everything. To talk, for freedom, for friends, to be alone. And I do so long . . . to cry! I feel as if I'm going to burst, and I know that it would get better with crying; but I can't, I'm restless, I go from one room to the other, breathe through the crack of a closed window, feel my heart beating, as if it is saying, 'Can't you satisfy my longings at last?' I believe that it's Spring within me, I feel that Spring is awakening, I feel it in my whole body and soul. It is an effort to behave normally, I feel utterly confused, don't know what to read, what to write, what to do, I only know that I am longing.*
>
> The Diary of Anne Frank

HUMAN LONELINESS

No person has ever walked our earth and been free from the pains of loneliness. Rich and poor, wise and ignorant, faith-filled and agnostic, healthy and unhealthy, have all alike had to face and struggle with its potentially paralysing grip. It has granted no immunities. To be human is to be lonely . . . Even if you are a relatively happy person, a person who relates easily to others and has many close friends, you are probably still lonely at times. If you are a very sensitive person, the type who feels things deeply, you are probably, to some degree, lonely all the time.

RONALD ROLHEISER: *The Restless Heart*

I only know that I am longing. It is one of the hardest things to do, to identify the cause of our restlessness, to find the root of our dissatisfaction. We know that what we long for is God and that we cannot find rest except in him – but what is it that only God can give us?

I believe our longings are a symptom of our loneliness, a condition from which none of us is exempt. It is not a condition that can be measured by the yardstick of friends or colleagues, neighbours or even family. Marriages can fall apart after years and years, often leaving one or both partners puzzled and shocked – I thought I really *knew* that person! Sometimes living in close proximity to another can actually highlight loneliness.

What we are longing for most of all is intimacy, to be *known* intimately as we really are. Yet we can be frozen up inside, quite unable to let others really know us, not least for fear of rejection. I once heard loneliness described as living with the pain of your own beauty, the frustration of perhaps sub-consciously knowing that we are lovable – that is, able to be loved – and longing to give this gift of ourselves to others, for our longing for love is rooted just as much in giving it as receiving it. But the sheer complexity of relationship in the world we have to live in seems to leave us, in the words of Isaiah, 'storm-tossed and disconsolate' (54: 11).

People pay thousands of pounds to psychiatrists, sometimes simply to get a hearing, just to find one person in the world who will listen. But though therapy can take people a long way towards self-acceptance, it can never go all the way, because all the way is loving and only God can take us along the final stretch of total self-giving that enables us to give and receive pure love. When we come to terms with that, then we are be-ginning to get in touch with what the spiritual life is all about.

Our longing, and our loneliness, are our opportunities to respond. Prayer is the response – not just cheaper than psychoanalysis, it's totally free! 'Let the man who is thirsty come to me' says Jesus. 'Anyone who drinks the water that I shall give will never be thirsty again' (John 4: 14). The choice is ours: to live as best we can with the shadows of love, with all the compromises and disappointments, or to venture like Abraham into the uncharted country of prayer and allow God to weld my heart to his own, and thus to others.

> No amount of partying and drinking, pleasure and travel, fame and fortune, success and creativity, indeed no amount of genuine human love and affec-tion, can ever fully take our loneliness away. All of these things are good in themselves and can even help somewhat to alleviate our loneliness. But God has made us bigger than human love and affection. Only a total all-encompassing consummate union with all sincere persons, the world and with the divine life itself will finally put to rest our last lonely impulse.
> RONALD ROLHEISER: *The Restless Heart*

THE MODERN MALAISE

If I were called upon to identify briefly the principal trait of the entire twentieth century, I would be unable to find anything more precise than to repeat: 'men have forgotten God'. The failings of human consciousness, deprived of its divine dimension, have been a determining factor in all the major crimes of this century.

ALEXANDER SOLZHENITSYN

The above words are taken from Alexander Solzhenitsyn's acceptance speech for the Templeton Prize for religion. This was a man who had lived through an era that had seen the implementation of one of the great social theories, who had suffered from it and who had survived to witness what he called its bankruptcy. But whereas communism had deliberately set out to abolish 'the divine dimension', the problem was just as acute elsewhere: it had simply disappeared through neglect. God had been forgotten, and his appeal to the West – indeed the world – was to rediscover this 'consciousness of a creator of all'.

What has happened, then, to eclipse so thoroughly this awareness of the divine? What preoccupations have obscured it? It seems to me there are two factors, and the first in a word is speed. Speed, paradoxically, has crept up on us and taken our lives over. In themselves the achievements of progress are good, God-given, and there is no denying there is joy and freedom to be found in our conquest of time and distance. The danger comes when speed becomes an end in itself, and a ground swell of frantic activity engulfs us. Life *has* become high-speed. If an advertiser wants to sell a product, then it must be time-saving, labour-saving or better still, instant. If, God forbid, you have time on your hands there are plenty of items ready to fill it. Credit cards can even take the waiting out of wanting, for we all know waiting is anathema. We cannot deny that in this century we have moved into and are now permanently settled down to living in the fast lane. Take my own subject, cooking: there was a time when the ingredients married together during the cooking time and deliciously developed flavour and aroma, but microwave ovens have put paid to all that because it all takes far too long!

As if it wasn't enough that speed has overwhelmed us and become second nature, what about that other subtle evil – noise? We are woken up by clock radios (depriving us of those few precious reflective moments between sleeping and waking), and noise then follows us around for the rest of the day, piped into supermarkets, pubs, stations. We take it around with us in personal stereos, except that they are anything but personal. Television and radio programmes span the clock, not always listened to but switched on just for a steady input of noise. I used to enjoy the space of the train journey to London from home but now people sit making and receiving phone calls on portable phones all the way! What we have to live with in modern society are, in effect, wall-to-wall distractions. We are cramming in twice as much noise and activity into our daily lives as our ancestors did. They sat and darned socks, walked from one place to another, and only communicated long distance by letter. Nowadays the world is far too *busy* to watch a sunset and remember God. We suffer a weakened sense of the contemplative experiences of life which occur in those ordinary daily events and touch us at a deeper level, enlivening our sense of the spiritual. All the time what we are craving from our frenetic activity is *experience* and yet this is the very thing that deprives us and diminishes our spiritual development and potential.

Of course God *is* still in evidence in all the bustle and noise and in all the media of communication that surround us: yes of course these are all part of his creation. But it is *we* who are moving too fast to see him and too drowned in noise to hear him.

> *'Martha, Martha,'* he said, *'you worry and fret about so many things; and yet few are needed, indeed only one . . .'*
>
> LUKE 10: 42

THE CURE

All the troubles of life come upon us because we refuse to sit quietly for a while each day in our rooms.

PASCAL

If our modern obsession with speed and noise is what is responsible for the stifling of the contemplative side of our nature – and I am convinced it is – then it requires no great intellectual feat to conclude that what's needed to redress the balance is the opposite of these two: namely, stillness and silence.

As a contemporary echo of Pascal's wise words above, one American psychiatrist stated recently he believed he could cure ninety per cent of mental illness if only he could persuade his patients to spend thirty minutes a day being still and silent. Be that as it may, it is still a striking commentary on the billions of pounds spent every year on analysis, anti-depressants or tranquillisers. Why, the very word tranquillise is a giveaway: if only we knew *how* to be tranquil we would surely not need such things.

This is not to suggest that tranquillity itself is a cure-all. In the 1960s there was a fashionable enthusiasm for something called transcendental meditation. Young people saw the need to opt out of the pressures of life, to reach for something beyond them. The reason it did not provide any lasting solutions was that it offered a misconceived (certainly, for a Christian) idea of what prayer is. To transcend means to go beyond the range of human experience, but Christianity (like Jesus himself) is rooted in the experience of ordinary life; here, and only here, can we meet God and experience him.

[145]

Transcendentalism and the 'techniques' associated with it involve a person being centred on themselves, which is the antithesis of Christian prayer. Actually trying to empty the mind requires a great deal of effort and this can even be another form of busy-ness. As human beings we're not all meant to scale the highest peaks. But with desire, dedication and practice it *can* be done. So can emptying the mind, but for what purpose and to what end? Absolutely none as far as prayer is concerned. Because God gave me a mind to think with, emptying it will give me nothing but a sense of achievement for which I will have expended much time and effort – or if I don't achieve it, a very human headache.

The true object of being still and silent is to become *receptive*, to allow another – God – to accomplish something within, to awaken a person to that deeper level of existence which is no more than a whisper in a strident world. In stillness and silence we begin to tune in to the wavelength of that hidden presence which is not stifled and obstructed by the world's speed and noise and what Newman called the 'fever of life'.

> *May He support us all day long, till the shadows lengthen and the evening comes, and the busy world is hushed, and the Fever of Life is over, and our work is done! Then in His mercy, may He give us safe lodging, and a holy rest and peace at the last.*

J. H. NEWMAN: *Sermon 1834*

TRUTH AND SOLITUDE

I discover more and more each day my need for these times of solitude in which I can rediscover others with more truth, and accept in the light of God my own weakness, ignorance, egoism and fear. This solitude does not separate me from others: it helps me love them more tenderly, realistically and attentively. I begin to distinguish between the false solitude which is a flight from others to be alone with egoism, sadness and a bruised sensitivity, and true solitude which is a communion with God and others.

JEAN VANIER: *Community and Growth*

To find that elusive stillness and silence we need solitude – but straightaway that needs to be clarified. For there is the wrong kind of solitude, the kind that can simply become an excuse for escaping from people. As the quote above explains, finding solitude should not mean separation from the world. People always need people: each of us is a part of the whole; even those who have a vocation to a solitary life of prayer (and that is rare enough anyway) have to be in some way serving others. Whether it's through their hours of prayer for the world or their preaching or writing, somehow the life of intercession should be fruitful for others and flow out to them.

Prayer cannot be an escape from life: it should in fact expand people's capacity for the experience of life and others, focusing people away from self. A mind freed from pressures can see that much more clearly the wonder of creation, like Wordsworth rejoicing at the sight of daffodils which 'flash upon that inward eye/Which is the bliss of solitude'.

A Journey into God

What stillness and silence do is to help us reflect at a deeper level, to get in touch with our inner selves, which are really our true selves. We can only do this in solitude because the rest of our lives are conducted at a completely different, if you like surface, level. There our lives are governed by feelings, the daily complexities of living are dealt with by instant decisions or emotional responses, and we find ourselves so often blown like leaves along a path by the winds of the world's bustle. As we career along, can we really be having a true say in what we're doing or where we're going? When the answer is no, perhaps it's because people have lost touch with their true selves and I feel sure this is the cause of many a breakdown, depression or mid-life crisis.

The desire to pray, I'm sure, is really an acknowledgment that life does operate on these two levels. It is also a desire to get the balance between them right, the ideal being to live as it were from the inside out, looking and reflecting on life from the deep centre of truth – rather than living from the outside in, only ever experiencing the surface level. Perhaps the best way of describing this comes from the Book of Wisdom, which tells us of God's gift of a 'thinking heart'. That is what allows us to be happy with our human limitations and in the end becomes a communion. In stillness and silence I wait on God who 'enlightens the eyes of my mind', which in turn enables me to live in truth and give myself more truly to others.

> *To go up alone into the mountain and to come back as an ambassador to the world has ever been the method of humanity's best friends.*

EVELYN UNDERHILL

CHAPTER EIGHT

What is Prayer?

LOVE ALONE

'Master, which is the greatest commandment of the Law?' Jesus said, 'You must love the Lord your God, with all your heart, with all your soul and with all your mind. This is the greatest and the first commandment. The second resembles it: You must love your neighbour as yourself. On these two commandments hang the whole Law, and the Prophets also.'

MATTHEW 22: 36–40

I would maintain that if anyone wanted a précis of the Bible in one paragraph, the verses above would suffice just on their own. Jesus is distilling the whole of the Old Testament Scriptures into a single word: love. *You must love* is what God's entire programme for the world is about.

If we examine the text closely, it seems to me that while it contains two 'commandments' it actually offers three lessons in loving. We should love God, love others and equally we should love ourselves. This last one, love of self, is sometimes left unconsidered, yet it is inextricably bound up with the other two in a pattern of interaction as follows: if I draw nearer to God (through prayer), then I begin to expose myself to his love. The beginning and end of prayer is learning to be receptive, learning not only what love is but also that I am loved. It is like the baby passively receiving his mother's loving smiles and gradually, without making it happen, understanding a mother's love (see page 20).

When I come to perceive in prayer, however gradually, God's unique love for me then I can begin to accept and love myself, which is a landmark stage in loving because then I can look beyond myself and not only reciprocate God's love but turn towards others in love also. It's a strange process in many ways but every level of self-acceptance frees us from self-focus and this in turn enables us to really look at others, to really see perhaps for the first time their struggles and problems as well as their joys. Having accepted ourselves with all our weaknesses and failures, suddenly we are quite happy to accept everyone else. It is a natural progression, indeed the only possible one. We cannot actually force ourselves to love; but if we have learned how to receive God's love, and love and value ourselves, then truly loving others will never be a problem.

But how, we want to know, can I receive this love? With patience and trust is the answer, for the truth is – in St Paul's famous five-word sentence – 'it is all God's work' (2 Corinthians 5: 18). Prayer is a waiting game, being prepared to wait for what I don't yet know to be revealed to me. It is human nature to want to know everything and to know it *now* – not much has changed since Adam and Eve – and the rational mind naturally recoils from the suggestion that I can't procure it for myself: surely if I read the right books or find the right guru I can do away with this tedious waiting?

No, the tiny infant which is our spiritual life has to remain helpless, open only to the instilling of love silently and imperceptibly, and allowing it to work its own way to growth and fulfilment.

> *If I have all the eloquence of men or of angels but speak without love, I am simply a gong booming or a cymbal clashing. If I have the gift of prophecy, understanding all the mysteries there are and knowing everything, and if I have faith in all its fullness to move mountains, but without love, then I am nothing at all . . . There are three things that last: faith, hope and love; and the greatest of these is love.*

1 CORINTHIANS 13: 1–3, 13

PRAYER IS RELATIONSHIP

The nearer you go to God, the nearer he will come to you.

JAMES 4: 8

It has occurred to me in the course of writing this book to drop the word prayer altogether, and replace it with the word relationship. Prayer has the inevitable connotations of asking, please say a prayer for me, pray for my exam, pray for a parking space, pray the soufflé will rise; whereas relationship is something quite different, it describes a state of being. As we have seen, God's plan for the human race is love, but to arrive at a state of love we need to work backwards, as it were, and find out how love is possible in human terms and through human means, since this is the nature of our creation and our only way to God.

How do people come to love one another? The first stage of love is knowing someone. Of course we all *say* we love people we don't really know: the Queen, the President, a pop-star, a sportsman. I can parade a T-shirt proclaiming 'I love J.R.' but it isn't really love, only a feeling somewhere on the spectrum between approval and hero-worship. The reason I can't really love J.R. or the President is that I don't really know them. How much of our shallow loving falls by the wayside when we *do* get to know people! I have been at Christian conferences where the emotional temperature of 'loving' has soared to ethereal heights, but in truth the people attending are still strangers.

To really love another you have to know them intimately: this is why anxious parents wisely plead with impetuous couples not to marry in haste 'because you hardly know each other'.

[153]

Far from being blind, love is only possible with wide-open eyes. Which takes us further back to another precondition for love; that is, in order to get to know someone you must spend time with that person, serious time, prime time. If I spend half an hour a day talking and listening to someone (even on the phone) then I can begin to relate to them, but a once-a-year conversation is no basis for any relationship.

If I *wish* to enter into this programme of loving which God has revealed in the Scriptures then it begins with time, time in which I get to know this God who longs to give me his love. Is not intimacy what we all long for, rather than the half-listening, self-absorbed relationships we normally encounter? Prayer is a very serious relationship and a real commitment to know God who then ceases to be a distant idol or a mild flirtation or just someone to unload all my news and requests or polite list of thank yous on to.

Like any human relationship it will grow and develop: there is no such thing as instant intimacy. There will be high spots and low spots, sometimes feeling, sometimes lack of feeling. But like a human relationship, where acquaintance matures into companionship and then into commitment, it is time spent together away from the crowds that creates the bond of intimacy – being present solely for each other. True love cannot exist without that intimate knowledge that inspires mutual trust, and a union so close that two individuals are one: one mind, one flesh, one love.

> *Prayer activity can be no substitute for time set aside exclusively for God. How sad it is that prayer in this sense is not part and parcel of the normal Christian life, and yet without it one cannot be fully Christian.*

> RUTH BURROWS: *Guidelines to Mystical Prayer*

WHAT HAVE YOU TO DO WITH YOUR PRECIOUS TIME?

O you who were created for union with God himself and whom he is ever attracting to himself, what are you doing with your precious lives, with your time? You are labouring for nothingness and all you think you possess is pure misery. O terrible human blindness. So great a light about you and you do not see it, so clear a voice sounding and you do not hear it.

ST JOHN OF THE CROSS: *Spiritual Canticle 39*

If we continue, for a moment, to follow our human couple and the pattern of their relationship, one thing is clear: the relationship exists only because they have *chosen* each other. That choice is then substantiated by a commitment – in the marriage ceremony they make vows to be committed to one another whatever happens. Do you take this person? – I do. Will you love this person? – I will.

Prayer, our relationship with God, involves the same choice. I choose to pray or not to pray: the decision is mine and mine alone. Yet it is a decision made not for any other specific aim, but to make a commitment to God, to devote say thirty minutes of my time each day to a relationship with him. I may have no idea what I am entering into, but no more did Abraham when he set out to an unknown country – yet there must have been for him that moment of decision to up and leave and take his chances. I remember only too well when I was first asked to do a television series on cooking, I had no idea how to go about it, or whether I could even do it at all. There aren't any schools to teach you that sort of thing, so I simply had to decide if I *wanted* to do it and then learn as I went along.

Prayer is exactly the same – you learn on the way. When someone says I can't pray, what they often mean is I've decided not to. If I desperately want to pass a driving test or gain a university degree or win a race, I *will* devote myself to lessons or study or training. People expend themselves and devote their energies precisely in accordance with their desires. So with prayer, the fundamental question is: do I want to know God?

There will always be a hundred and one reasons why I don't have thirty minutes a day to spare, but each one of those reasons should be examined in the light of that fundamental question. How long does it take to read a newspaper, read a novel, weed the garden? How many hours of television or radio 'occupy' me every week? Am I satisfying myself with a measure of good works that can be nodded in the direction of God? But God may not want a catalogue of good works. He *does* want love, and loving needs time off the treadmill.

So what, then, are we doing with our precious time? Am I slaving away through a sense of guilt or driving myself furiously through lack of self-esteem? What – we must ask ourselves – is it in my daily round that gives me life, that enables me to give and receive the love that is the sole purpose of my creation? Who is it that can set me free, give me peace, heal my blindness, open my ears? Answer these questions honestly and there is a basis for a decision and a commitment.

When you have to make a choice and don't make it,
that is in itself a choice.
WILLIAM JAMES

THE PRACTICALITIES OF PRAYER

'You must come away to some lonely place all by yourselves and rest awhile'; for there were so many coming and going that the apostles had no time even to eat. So they went off in a boat to a lonely place where they could be by themselves.

MARK 6: 31

Having made a decision – yes, I *want* to know God through a commitment to prayer – sooner or later one has to face up to the practical side of what is involved. How easily we can identify with the apostles, knowing what it's like having people 'coming and going' the whole time! Even if we did have a boat handy, how can we ever begin to find time for God in our pressured lives? Well, here I can only speak from personal experience, but at least with the benefit of having to combine full-time work with running a home (and perhaps I could also add that public life also brings a few extra headaches as well!).

Habit, Aristotle said, is second nature, and I'm convinced that is what prayer has to become: habit, something that I will come to take for granted, as natural a part of life as cleaning one's teeth. But forming a habit of prayer is something else, and will depend on an individual's circumstances – even, I suspect, their metabolism. It seems to me God created two distinct species, morning people and evening people. The first leap bright-eyed from their beds ready for the day, but tend to go down along with the sun; the second are incoherent before mid-morning but are bouncing by midnight! I make the point because, unless you are lucky enough to have a regular free

[157]

time during the day, the logical time to make 'space for God' is by getting up half an hour earlier or going to bed half an hour later. Whichever, it is important to acquire the habit of setting aside the same period each day.

A new habit has to be worked at, and there's no need to feel discouraged – an American psychologist has asserted it takes two years to form a new habit! The important thing is to persevere, and there is some consolation in the fact that, unlike other disciplines which demand great willpower or energy like dieting or jogging, the habit of prayer is restfully therapeutic. When the habit begins to stick, it will become something I quite naturally need, not something I force myself into.

What I am essentially doing is coming into God's presence for half an hour, giving that time totally to him. But because God is spirit and I am distinctly flesh-and-blood, it is helpful to have a suitable environment, a 'lonely place' specifically created for stillness and silence – the corner of a bedroom perhaps. Equally it is useful to have some tangible reminder of what this time represents, a crucifix or a favourite picture with a religious theme or even just a lighted candle.

I am just as sure a comfortable chair is needed, though perhaps the only other 'prop' that I would recommend from my experience might seem a little odd. I always have a watch or clock to hand, because trying to guess how long half an hour is is a real distraction. To start with, people unused to being still and silent may find the hands moving excruciatingly slowly, and five minutes turning into an age. But take heart. You *are* only human! One of the greatest writers on prayer, Teresa of Avila, used an hour-glass in the beginning and found herself shaking it to try to get the sand through more quickly!

> *Come to me all you who labour and are overburdened, and I will give you rest. Shoulder my yoke and learn from me, for I am gentle and humble in heart, and you will find rest for your souls. Yes, my yoke is easy and my burden light.*

MATTHEW 11: 28–30

SONG OF SERENITY

O Lord, my heart is not proud, nor haughty my eyes. I have not gone after things too great nor marvels beyond me. Truly I have set my soul in silence and peace; a weaned child on its mother's breast, even so is my soul.

PSALM 130/131: 1–2

The essential simplicity of prayer lies not just in the fact that it is a relationship, but in the nature of that relationship. What God has always been offering – as we saw when we looked at the history of his covenant promise – is a close and familiar relationship, which calls not for complex or sophisticated responses but quite the opposite.

First we can dispense with what are called techniques. There are a myriad instructions on the art of prayer, but prayer is not an art but an attitude. Jesus says, when you pray say 'Our Father', and although he threw in alongside a collection of subjects we are to pray for, what he was fundamentally saying was that your attitude to prayer should be like that of a child towards a father.

Let's imagine for a moment a father sitting in his study, and a child coming in from school to spend half an hour or so with dad – and see how incongruous 'techniques' would be. The child is in the presence of the father and the father in the presence of the child. Does the child need to sit in the lotus position? Does it need to breathe deeply in order to relax? Does it need to mutter repetitive phrases in order to be fully present to its father?

There is a danger in investing the subject of prayer with irrelevant technicalities: they may help some people to feel good, but they can just as easily drive others away. The Gospels could not have put it more simply: Jesus went off to a quiet place to be alone with his Father. It was not, to use the vernacular, a 'big deal'. God may well do great things in us – he almost certainly will – but for our part it is simply a matter of handing ourselves over to him.

Of course some of the great spiritual writers have explored the subject deeply, charting the various stages of development in prayer – and someone of an analytical mind may well be interested in such expositions. But relationship is not a matter of expertise in the end. I'm perfectly happy to switch on my television and watch satellite pictures live from America: the fact that I haven't a clue how the set works or the pictures are relayed does not prevent me from receiving the information or gaining enjoyment. Prayer is precisely the same – you really can short-circuit the analysis and just settle down to enjoy a relationship with a loving Father.

The psalm at the beginning repays deep reflection, because it sums up the most reassuring aspect of prayer. A weaned child has no motive for being there, has no special proficiency, no technique to employ: it just rests in silence and peace. I find it one of the most comforting images of prayer in the Bible, not only for anyone embarking on the journey of prayer but also as a reminder of its truth in times of difficulty.

> *And when you pray, do not imitate the hypocrites: they love to say their prayers standing up in the synagogues and at the street corners for people to see them . . . But when you pray, go to your private room and, when you have shut your door, pray to your Father who is in that secret place.*

MATTHEW 6: 5–6

JESUS THE WAY

It is written in the prophets:
They will all be taught by God,
and to hear the teaching of the Father,
and learn from it,
is to come to me.

JOHN 6: 45

Let us return briefly to the earlier tête-à-tête between a child and her father (for in this instance she happens to be a girl!), and let us eavesdrop on what might be taking place between them. She listens to him, asks him questions, learns something. She may also learn simply by observing him, growing imperceptibly in the same likeness. On the other hand she might be full of what has happened at school, and want to talk about it. Sometimes there is no conversation at all: he does the crossword, she plays with her dolls. Occasionally even there might be an argument, when she wants something badly and he won't let her have it.

Whatever the scenario, the important thing is that they are spending time together; for the child it is a time of development, of getting to know her father, his attitudes and opinions. His wisdom becomes her wisdom, and the bond of love grows stronger.

For the person first beginning to pray – to spend time with the Father – the wisdom is received through Scripture, the underpinning of all prayer. I would personally be even more specific and say the most important sections of Scripture for prayer are the Psalms and the Gospels. The Psalms are the greatest prayerbook of all because they embody the whole range of human experience, and can express a person's feelings very powerfully – the yearning or anger, despair or joy. But even more important are the Gospels, for in the life of Jesus we have *all* the teaching God wants to give us.

'To hear the teachings of the Father is to come to me' means precisely that. There are an infinite number of books written, tapes produced, sermons delivered on prayer but while they can be useful aids, they can never replace the pure teaching which God reveals to us through the Gospels. They never lose their relevance, speaking afresh from age to age, individual to individual in an extraordinarily direct and personal way.

'Show us the Father' asked Philip the disciple 'and we shall be satisfied.' 'To have seen me is to have seen the Father' comes the reply. 'I am in the Father and the Father is in me' (John 14). It is in reflecting on the Gospels that we learn to say 'Our Father' because we begin to understand who he is and what he means. This reflecting on the Gospels cannot be bypassed: we need to be *infused* with their message, to hear everything Jesus said and everything he did so that, albeit unconsciously, we begin to hear the teaching of the Father and grow in the likeness of God himself.

> *A child of God listens to the words of God;*
> *if you refuse to listen,*
> *it is because you are not God's children.*

JOHN 8: 47

THE PSYCHOLOGY OF PRAYER

> *I cannot understand my own behaviour. I fail to carry out the things I want to do and I find myself doing the very things I hate . . . The fact is, I know of nothing good living in me – living, that is, in my unspiritual self – for though the will to do what is good is in me, the performance is not.*

ROMANS 7: 15, 18

Getting to what it is we truly want is handicapped by our own complex, many-layered make-up, our 'unspiritual selves' which can lay down a smokescreen to deflect us from our true aim. I believe that the only resource that we have to penetrate these complexities is a *genuine desire* for a relationship with God.

These psychological diversions on our journey of prayer have to be encountered head-on. One of them – certainly not the least – is that inevitable list of reasons we summon up as to why we can't pray or give time to God just now. However let's put it into perspective: if I enjoy watching a certain regular television programme, say *Dallas* on Wednesday or *This Week* on Thursday or *The South Bank Show* on Sunday, I can be pretty certain I shan't find any reasons against it. It will actually be perfectly easy, just switch on the TV and sit and watch! Likewise with any activity where there will be a certain amount of guaranteed satisfaction.

When it comes to prayer (or more specifically, setting aside time for prayer) it will be amazing how much pressing business will require my urgent attention *now*. Any journalist or writer will know what I mean, because until the deadline is imminent everything under the sun has to be done before any actual words get written – floors scrubbed, phone calls made, dogs walked, you name it.

The problem with prayer is there's no built-in deadline to force us into self-discipline. Therefore we have mentally to prepare ourselves to deal logically with this 'spontaneous' list of duties. If, like me, you tend to be a little absent-minded, simply write them down, examine the list and ask yourself what really cannot wait half an hour. The answer will always be, nothing. That will be one little psychological victory you can chalk up.

But be on your guard at this point. I have been known to be actually on my way to spend time in prayer and have suddenly noticed a plant which is in danger of immediate death if water is not supplied within the next few seconds! Now where did I put that special plant-waterer – it's not in its usual place. It is discovered after ten minutes' search and water is forthcoming, and the water left in the container is then distributed among other dying plants. After which the phone rings ... the prayer-time has slipped away for good, through no fault of mine of course.

Self-discipline needs determination, which only our real deepest desire for God can fortify. Sooner or later the habit will have instilled itself when we can apply our mental 'blinkers' to all irrelevancies and keep our minds focused only on that precious time we set aside for prayer.

> *If the Lord does not build the house,*
> *in vain do its builders labour ...*
> *in vain is your earlier rising*
> *and going later to rest.*
> *You who toil for the bread you eat,*
> *when he pours gifts on his beloved while they slumber.*

PSALM 126/127: 1–2

CHAPTER NINE

It's all God's Work!

SPECIAL RELIGIOUS EXPERIENCES

Let us remind ourselves over and over again that holiness has to do with very ordinary things: *truthfulness, courtesy, kindness, gentleness, consideration for others, contentment with our lot, honesty and courage in the face of life, reliability, dutifulness.*

RUTH BURROWS: *Interior Castle Explored* (my emphasis)

In this passage Ruth Burrows has encapsulated precisely what the Scriptures say about holiness, which is to say that you know the soundness of a tree by the fruit it produces. Holiness is to be found in everyday life. It is utterly false to measure the presence of God's influence in a person's life by the yardstick of any kind of religious experience.

Here, I think, a distinction has to be made. We need to appreciate that some people have quite natural psychic gifts. My grandmother, with her Celtic perceptiveness, would suddenly announce that we should 'expect visitors', and sure enough visitors arrived! Personally I think this is no different from other gifts of sensitivity which countless other people possess (though they may lead them to pursue a career telling fortunes at the end of Brighton pier or bending spoons on television), and in the end is no more extraordinary than a gift for music or mental arithmetic.

Where we need to reach for the warning button is when this

gets grafted onto religion, when someone with psychic gifts claims exclusive religious experiences, be they dreams, visions, ecstasies or whatever. Such claims can very often imply that not only are they in receipt of signs and wonders attributed to God, but that he has bestowed his special favour upon certain people whom he has chosen to raise up above the rest of the pack.

Not only does this diminish God, it is quite contrary to the universality of the gospel teaching: '*anybody* who loves me will be loved by my Father' (John 14: 21). It is perfectly incongruous that God could only reveal himself to a favoured few. It is also, I'm afraid, insidious because when some claim to have privileged information and special access to God denied to the rest, it can make others feel second-class in their own search for God. I speak with feeling on this point, for there was a stage in my life when – although I knew deep-down that no one is more special to God than anyone else – I began to feel that, since others seemed to be so persuasive about their 'special experiences', there must be something wrong with me and the barrenness of my prayer. (I would add that it was reading the books of Ruth Burrows that helped to put the problem into perspective for me.)

I understand now that, in some cases, it was some form of intuition being mistakenly communicated as divine writ, as 'God told me' so and so. Such insights which can lead us to the truth are common to all, but emphasis on the extraordinary in prayer is a perversion of prayer. It is a form of being self-focused, and that can be an escape from God. When we genuinely present ourselves to God, he never fails to meet us and influence us in our ordinary daily experiences of living. These and only these are the true signs.

> *What the Spirit brings is ... love, joy, peace, patience, kindness, goodness, trustfulness, gentleness and self-control.*
>
> GALATIANS 5: 22

RULES AND REGULATIONS

One of the Pharisees invited him to a meal. When he arrived at the Pharisee's house and took his place at table, a woman came in, who had a bad name in the town. She had heard he was dining with the Pharisee and had brought with her an alabaster jar of oint-ment. She waited behind him at his feet, weeping, and her tears fell on his feet, and she wiped them away with her hair; then she covered his feet with kisses and anointed them with the ointment. When the Pharisee who had invited him saw this, he said to himself, 'If this man were a prophet, he would know who this woman is that is touching him and what a bad name she has.'

LUKE 7: 36–9

This story vividly illustrates how prayer can be hedged about by an invisible barrier of religious rules and regulations. This Pharisee personifies the institutionalised belief that outside the letter of the law all is lost: *his* message is, repent or else! The irony was that he was implying this to Jesus, whose very name in Hebrew embodied the message of salvation – 'Yahweh saves'. It is God who saves *us* from our self-centredness and our mixed-up motives in seeking him. Yet what happens so often is that this is turned on its head, so that it would appear that we are to save ourselves first before we can approach God.

We should be careful not to get caught up in the whiter-than-white brand of spirituality. Prayer is not a moral statement, but a plea for help. I don't pray because I've reached a certain stage of moral perfection, thanking God 'I'm not like other men'. I pray because I'm a lousy crumb, but have reached a painful stage of wisdom – which is knowing that I can't actually do anything myself about it.

In prayer God meets us in our humanity, and the work of transforming that humanity into divinity is his. I can give all I possess to the poor, visit the sick, never step out of line or ever commit a serious sin, but I can be a million miles from God and not be letting him anywhere near me because I am caught up in the pride of achievement. The finger-pointers like the Pharisee are usually the ones who are furthest from him.

The woman in the story was under no illusions as to what kind of person she was. One of the most significant details in the story is her unwillingness to let him see her: she waited *behind* him, denoting the poorest self-image, as it were a spiritual disfigurement. Yet her tears, I feel, are not a symptom of self-focused depression but a normal reaction to encountering the healing that goes hand-in-hand with the pain of knowing what it is to be human in a fallen world. She could so easily have avoided the Pharisee's house, and chosen to remain a victim of her disastrous life. She could never have known that gentle forgiving love had she not drawn near.

How many people, I wonder, never draw near enough to God because they simply don't feel good enough? Those who have experienced rejection often feel, quite mistakenly, it is their fault. Those who struggle with sinfulness can be prey to the finger-pointers, preaching their rules and regulations and driving them further still from the God of mercy and compassion. This woman's story is universal: we are only able to understand unconditional love if we choose to draw near and receive it.

> *Then Jesus took him up and said, 'Simon, I have something to say to you'. 'Speak, Master' was the reply. 'There was once a creditor who had two men in his debt; one owed him five hundred denarii, the other fifty. They were unable to pay, so he pardoned*

*them both. Which of them will love him more?' 'The
one who was pardoned more, I suppose' answered
Simon. Jesus said, 'You are right'.*

LUKE 7: 40–3

GOD AT WORK

My Father goes on working, and so do I.

Not the easiest thing to come to terms with about prayer is that it is (in the words of St Paul which entitle this chapter) 'all God's work'. On the one hand this should be a tremendous relief to us; on the other hand we have this perennial problem of wanting to achieve rather than receive. While there is still a widespread belief that there is some knack to prayer, some secret method that brings results, it is always going to be difficult to grasp that our role in prayer is profoundly passive.

'But when you pray' Jesus said, 'go to your private room and, when you have shut your door, pray to your Father who is in that secret place' (Matthew 6: 6). That secret place, where God 'works' within me, is not just secret from the world, it is also in a sense secret from me. It is the deep centre of my being, where God's activity is beyond my conscious perception. Ah! you may say, but Jesus promised that whoever follows him will *not* walk in darkness but have the light of life for his guide. Is that not a contradiction?

No, prayer *is* darkness to me (or what St John of the Cross calls 'night to my senses'). The hallmark of my prayer is not what does or does not happen in my prayer-time: the question of experience or non-experience is simply not relevant. The evidence will become apparent in the events of daily life. The light of life is perceived in the fruits of prayer, in spiritual growth.

[172]

This is not to suggest that my life is going to grow instantly in perfection. I am not going to grow immune to the turmoil, conflicts or disappointments of the world. I am not going to shrug off the imperfections of my own nature through prayer. But there *can* be peace within turmoil, love beneath the conflicts, and joy in spite of the disappointments. It is a gradually changing perspective, rather than a personality transplant.

What we have begun to do is what St Paul says and that is to 'have the mind of Christ' (1 Corinthians 2: 16). What prayer should be doing is shifting me in my values, instilling a wisdom I could never acquire for myself. Ultimately this process will become realised in my life, but not through trying to analyse what happens to me 'in secret', rather by surrendering to God at work (so much easier, for a start!). God always fulfils his work in those who allow him to do so.

What is born of the flesh is flesh;
what is born of the Spirit is spirit.
Do not be surprised when I say:
You must be born from above.
The wind blows wherever it pleases;
you hear its sound,
but you cannot tell where it comes from or where it is
going.
That is how it is with all those who are born of the
Spirit.

JOHN 3: 6–8

WHEN WE KNOW IT NOT

If thou appear untouched by solemn thought,
Thy nature is not therefore less divine.
Thou liest in Abraham's bosom all the year;
And worshipp'st at the temple's inner shrine,
God being with thee when we know it not.

WILLIAM WORDSWORTH

Wordsworth's sonnet, in praise of a 'beauteous evening', is one of his most eloquent descriptions of God revealed in nature. At that moment of sunset it is possible to view the natural world as 'breathless in adoration' and to see the 'gentleness of heaven'. At such moments our belief is reinforced by feelings and emotions. But most of us, for most of the time, are 'untouched by solemn thought'. At times in fact we may feel no desire at all for God or prayer, however beauteous the evening might be!

What we have to do is become reconciled to this lack of felt desire. Prayer can never be judged at the emotional level, whatever 'experiences' other people may claim. There may well be those who get breathless with adoration, but those who don't need have no fears. Prayer mirrors life: some days we feel good, on others we don't. There are sunny days when God's in his heaven and all's well with the world, and there are dull and drizzly days when we feel distinctly earthbound. Watching the sun go down on a palm-fringed beach with the waves gently lapping, I may well *feel* God is great. When my car has broken down in a thunderstorm and I'm miles from a phone, I may not *feel* he exists at all at that precise moment!

[174]

How can we base anything on the see-saw of emotion? How can we have any confidence in the permanence of our feelings? We can't. The permanence of reality lies deep down, at the 'inner shrine'. A marriage survives and matures not because of the intensity of emotion which may have marked the honeymoon, but because of a deep inner commitment.

When I go out and talk to people about prayer, I can see that they are visibly relieved and reassured when I tell them that I very rarely feel like praying (to be honest, I frequently don't feel like it). Sometimes I don't feel like being married, or working, or running a home. But I carry on doing all these things, knowing that I am committed to them, that I am committed because I made a choice, and that I made the choice because deep down that was what I wanted.

That is what matters in the end. We commit ourselves to prayer because at base we *want* to know God, and whether we feel good about it is quite irrelevant. What above all sustains us in our commitment is the fact that, wherever we may be on the feeling level, God is with us even 'when we know it not' as the poet points out. Like the bride in the Song of Songs we sleep though our hearts are awake: just being present to God in prayer is allowing him to continue working within us.

> *God is the still point at the centre.*
> *There is no doer but he.*
> *All this he showed me with great joy,*
> *saying 'See, I am God, See, I am in all things.*
> *See, I do all things.'*
> JULIAN OF NORWICH

WAITING ON GOD

I waited, I waited for the Lord
and he stooped down to me,
he heard my cry.
He drew me from the deadly pit, from the miry clay.
He set my feet upon a rock
and made my footsteps firm.
Happy the man who has placed his trust in the Lord.

PSALM 39/40: 2–3, 5

Receptivity – not the most attractive word in the language –
but one that in the context of prayer we cannot dispense with,
because it describes the first, conceivably the only, precondition that is necessary. According to the dictionary it means the
'readiness to receive' and so far as it goes that is an adequate
definition. But to understand the full *implications* of receptivity we should return to some of the imagery we looked at in
earlier reflections, in particular the Old Testament image of the
mother bird rearing her young. It is she who provides everything they need for sustenance until they are ready to take
wing: they simply wait in a state of readiness to receive. (In fact
those gaping, chirping throats might seem to be taking recep-
tiveness to extremes! But, in the mother's time, each gets what
it needs to grow.)

Being receptive to God means allowing him to work in his way,
and at his speed. Remember the exodus story: the people could
not refrain from anticipating what their needs were and then
complaining at the lack of fulfilment of those needs. The
Hebrews grew uncomfortable with their vulnerability, to the
point of forgetting the pain of slavery and wishing they were

back in Egypt. It seemed preferable at the time to having to wait for God all the time.

In Deuteronomy God explains that he led them into the wilderness precisely that they should learn, to make them understand that their need of God was the supreme need in their lives. Were they prepared to let him be God, which meant receiving the life he offered rather than doing their own thing? The key sentence is the one quoted by Jesus in Matthew's Gospel: 'Man does not live on bread alone, but on every word that comes from the mouth of God' (Matthew 4: 4). It took them forty years, trailing round the desert, to finally learn. 'I was training you as a man trains his child, to follow me and reverence me' (Deuteronomy 8: 5).

We, too, have to learn. In prayer we enter the same desert and wait for our sustenance. Our readiness to receive also means waiting on God, learning to know him and understand that he *will* provide. Our receptivity involves becoming vulnerable and allowing him to teach us. Such things are as hard for us as they were for the people of the Exodus, so hard that often we give up on prayer.

> *In God alone is my soul at rest,*
> *my help comes from him.*
> *He alone is my rock, my stronghold, my fortress:*
> *I stand firm.*
>
> PSALM 61/62: 2–3

THE ONLY WORK THE FATHER WANTS

Then they said to him, 'What must we do to do the works that God wants?' Jesus gave them this answer: 'This is working for God: you must believe in the one he has sent.'

JOHN 6: 28–9

It was not, I suspect, quite the answer that Jesus' questioners were expecting. They were asking what they had to *do* – go to church, maybe, say the creed, pay attention to the sermon. But those who are content merely to fulfil some list of requirements are simply flirting with the meaning of Christianity. It isn't deeds that God wants, but belief in Jesus, for that is the only way to know him. A lifetime of meditation without knowing who Jesus is would be futile. Without knowing Jesus there is no way we can comprehend God as spirit, because we are flesh.

In his mercy God became flesh so that we *can* know him. Through the Gospels we can see his life and hear his words, and so have indwelling in us the Holy Spirit who Jesus promised would teach us everything. If we raise objections like I don't understand the Gospels, they're out of date, or I don't like the language, what we really mean is that I don't *want* to know. The desire is everything. The Highway Code must be the world's most boring book, but I'll read it if I want to drive badly enough.

There was nothing equivocal about Jesus' reply. I simply cannot believe in what I don't know, and in the New Testament I have been provided with the means of knowing – not

just by the ancient authors of the books, but by the community
of believers who have lived and kept alive their message from
one generation to another.

It is still a common question on people's lips: what can I *do*? I
recall a lady coming up to me after a talk I gave on prayer some
five years ago with that very query. I explained that I believed
prayer needed a daily commitment of time, and I remember
stressing the value of listening rather than doing: listen attentively to the Gospels during this time and reflect on their
teaching. Very recently, five years on, she came to another talk
to tell me how she had actually experienced the one-to-one
teaching contained in the Scriptures, how she had really come
to understand what Jesus said in John's Gospel; that 'to hear
the teaching of the Father is to come to me' (John 6: 45).

What had been a revelation to her was her own passivity: yes,
it really was something she had *received*. Her experience – and
that of others too – is proof to me that it is not action that is
needed but desire: a desire that leads to a decision, which in
turn will lead to belief in the one who was sent. These are the
'works' God wants us to be getting on with.

> For the one who asks always receives, the one who
> searches always finds, the one who knocks will
> always have the door opened to him.
> LUKE 11: 10

THE TEEMING MIND

What man indeed can know the intentions of God?
Who can define the will of the Lord? The reasonings
of mortals are unsure and our intentions unstable,
for a perishable body presses down the soul and this
tent of clay weighs down the teeming mind . . . As
for your intention who could have learnt it had you
not granted wisdom and sent your Holy Spirit from
above?

WISDOM 9: 13–17

What are you thinking? we often ask someone, and get the reply 'Oh nothing . . .' Which is much more likely to mean they don't want to tell you, rather than their mind is a complete blank. For the fact is that our minds do teem from morning to night, with questions, decisions, calculations, observations (and probably all night with dreams, as well!). Sometimes our errant thoughts are a distraction to what we really ought to be concerned about, and therein lies one of the commonest anxieties about prayer. Distractions.

If I sit for thirty minutes in God's presence and my mind keeps wandering off to what I might be having for lunch or what I need to buy at the supermarket, I will come away without feeling I've achieved anything. My lack of concentration becomes not just a matter for self-reproach, but an excuse as well. But the truth of the matter is that this is another case of ego at work for, to put it bluntly, worry about distractions is self-centred and not God-centred. I can't pray because my mind is too distracted means I don't want to pray because I don't get anything for myself out of it.

It is a perfectly human need to feel, to be aware, to experience something in my prayer-time, but it is not relevant. God communicates himself at a *deeper level than my mind*, at the spiritual level which is untouched by feelings. The soul is the secret me, and the Spirit of God deals with the secret me, giving himself to the degree that I want him. 'Look, I am standing at the door, knocking. If one of you hears me calling and opens the door I will come in' (Revelation 3: 20). Our minds *may* be teeming, but we can still be present to God at the level at which he operates.

This is not to offer carte-blanche for devoting the time to thinking through a project and calling it prayer, or going for a sleep and calling it prayer. God reads our hearts and, though our minds may wander, or even if we do drop off, *if* our deepest intentions are for him, he will be the Lord of our prayer. Teresa of Avila offered some characteristically practical counsel on the subject, describing the mind as a mill-wheel for ever driven round and round. Let it, she says, let the mill just clack on and ignore it. Elsewhere she likens distracting thoughts to butterflies, and advises us to just let them flit in and flit out again, without worrying about them. If we want God, want to pray, then we must learn to live with distractions: let our minds teem away and just be present to him regardless.

Earlier in this book I likened our lives to a boat making for harbour, with our souls the sail filled out by God's Spirit. The sails will propel the boat whatever other activity is going on on board; the only requirement is that we make the decision to trim the sails so as to catch the wind – in other words that our hearts are responsive even if our minds are an ocean away.

> *Glory be to him whose power, working in us, can do infinitely more than we can ask or imagine.*

EPHESIANS 3: 20

[181]

CHAPTER TEN

The Listening Life

THE ONE THING NEEDED

*'Martha, Martha,' he said 'you worry and fret about
so many things, and yet few are needed, indeed only
one. It is Mary who has chosen the better part; it is
not to be taken from her.'*

LUKE 10: 41

How many of us could identify, privately at least, with
Martha? There was her sister just sitting at the feet of Jesus,
when there were so many important things to be done about
the house. Finally she explodes: tell her to help me! Though
gentle, Jesus' response is very specific. There is only one thing
that is 'necessary' – and that is to listen to the one whom God
sent, which is an integral part of prayer.

Of course it's important to get this in perspective. We are not
meant literally to drop everything in our lives and pray all day,
but it is certainly a question of priorities, an assessment of the
value of our activities. Martha would probably have been
amazed how much of her busy-ness was automatic, unques-
tioned and entirely dispensable. Routine has the deadening
effect of precluding time even to take a studied look at our life-
styles: indeed it denies any incentive to do so.

To break into the vicious circle calls for a measure of decisive-
ness. I'm sure the subject of prayer suffers from too much
gift-wrapping. What I personally needed in the beginning –
and was lucky enough to get – was advice from someone who
did not mince matters. How can I draw nearer to God? was my
question. Receive the eucharist and spend an hour a day in
prayer, was the emphatic reply. No compromises, simply the
undiluted truth.

In practice this did not mean grafting prayer-time onto an existing routine, piecing it together like a mosaic from all those reflective moments – train journeys, ironing, taking the dog for a walk – precious though they are. It meant sitting in stillness and silence for a time each day and doing precisely what Mary of Bethany did. We are not able, as she was, to sit at the feet of a visible God, but it is what we are doing in spirit: coming into the presence of someone whom we cannot see or touch, but whom we *know* is there.

Just as the choice has to be unequivocal, so has the commitment. Elsewhere I have likened the commitment to prayer to the commitment to a marriage: I will love for better or worse, richer or poorer, in sickness and in health – which is pretty comprehensive. The commitment to prayer needs to be just as comprehensive: my commitment continues whether I feel I'm benefiting or not, or growing or not. Regrettably the concept of commitment is fading from modern life and its importance urgently needs to be re-established. A marriage that 'didn't work out' was not a serious commitment. Likewise people who try prayer for a while and then give up are not really committed to it. True and total commitment make both relationships and prayer much, much easier to handle. That is the greatest help and encouragement I have to offer.

> *Faith is not a thing of the mind; it is not an intellectual certainty or a felt conviction of the heart. It is a sustained decision to take God with utter seriousness as the God of our Life.*

> RUTH BURROWS: *Our Father*

THE TEACHING WORD

If you make my word your home, you will indeed be
my disciples. You will learn the truth and the truth
will make you free.

JOHN 8: 31

Prayer always has to begin with a person learning how to be at home with the Gospels, for it is there only that we come into direct contact with our intimate teacher whose mandate 'learn from me' should infuse the whole of our search for God. In an earlier reflection (page 51) we discussed the word as 'creative', and even on a secular level we can see how this can happen, how philosophies get translated into a way of life and manifestos into political systems. God's word is profoundly more creative: to the degree we allow the teaching to penetrate our lives, so will we come to recognise the teacher himself – beyond the words of Scripture – in the whole of our daily experience.

It is possible (and the tendency does exist) to make as it were a monument out of the Scriptures, something to be learned by heart, transcribed into slogans or used to justify one's personal opinions. This is to render the word totally uncreative. Teaching is for living, and contemplation of the Scriptures can only have value if what is being contemplated is transformed into a response. At the other extreme there are those who would claim that prayerful reflection on the Scripture is a way to avoid the demands of real life. Deeds not thoughts, they say, are what counts. The litmus test of Christianity is how it works in action among other people.

True only up to a point. In reality the two things are inseparable. To be a Christian means to become a disciple of Christ, and discipleship is both listening and imitating. Trying to short-circuit the process diminishes what it means to bear the name Christian.

What we have to accept, through faith rather than through any felt conviction, is that God is closer to each of us than we are to ourselves, that his Spirit is present at our deepest centre. So we approach the Gospels not in the sense of 'bible-study' (there are other times, other places for that) but with an attitude of receptivity which will allow the words to touch us and do their creative work. That of course will be God's work, and if we want to come away from our times of reflection feeling *we* have got somewhere or done something we will find it difficult. Prayer-time is listening time, time we have to wait on God.

That means being bold enough to take a chance on pure faith and believe in his promises. The promises are clear enough. If you 'make my word your home', that is live within the context of the word, you will learn the truth. That's a promise. The truth will make you free. That's another promise. Our part is to let it happen: listen first, receive the teaching, then we have the freedom to fulfil our role as disciples.

> *At various times in the past and in various different ways, God spoke to our ancestors through the prophets; but in our own time, the last days, he has spoken to us through his Son, the Son that he has appointed to inherit everything and through whom he has made everything there is. He is the radiant light of God's glory and the perfect copy of his nature.*
>
> HEBREWS 1: 1–3

HEARING AND LISTENING

Listen, listen to me, and you will have good things to eat
and rich food to enjoy.
Pay attention, come to me;
listen, and your soul will live.

ISAIAH 55: 3

The Pharisees to whom Jesus was addressing this remark were, by all accounts, good talkers. Their religion embraced a great deal of talking, talking for the most part at God. It made them indifferent listeners, and anyone who's really interested in knowing God will want to listen to what *he* has to say. 'To hear the teaching of the Father . . . is to come to me' (John 6: 45) – so all of us have set before us the direct access to what God wants us to hear. But hearing and listening are by no means the same thing.

Listening is about wanting to hear. The Bible illuminatingly talks of the ear as a channel to the heart: it is in that channel that blockages occur, often normal human preoccupations that inhibit listening. We encountered earlier a 'teeming mind', and I really believe my own mind works overtime in teeming. I can read the same pages of a book several times without absorbing a word of them. I rarely manage to concentrate on the opening of a play or film. I am frequently jumping ahead of people's conversation in my mind, only to find myself embarrassed to have missed some vital point. I doubt that I am alone in this: a real talent for listening is a most loving gift to others.

In the normal pattern of our lives we hear a great deal, talks, conversations, radio programmes. We may even be mildly attentive, but only when something catches us do we prick up

[189]

our ears. When something resonates and awakens that 'really hearing' sensitivity, then we start listening. The same pattern will occur when we take a gospel passage to prayer and sit with it for a period. We may be only mildly attentive to it, it may even be the last thing we feel like doing. There may be passages that seem difficult, or mean nothing, or even seem alien to our thinking. But what we must be clear about is that God himself is our teacher, and it is his Spirit that awakens ours rather than our own anxious efforts to extract something meaningful. God *will* reach us but he will give us only what we are able to take at the time, little by little. It may be just a sentence, one word even, that touches us – and that will act as a springboard for reflection, perhaps offering enlightenment in some new way.

And what if we sometimes hear nothing? That's fine too, for it will at least be an exercise in self-giving which is what love is about. We all have friends whose conversation is sometimes hard going, but for love of them we don't get up and leave. Like all relationships prayer has its peaks and troughs, good days and bad, but if we don't feel anxious about it and keep listening, the truth *will* come to set us free.

> *Truth must find an echo in the one who hears it to be recognised. Put it another way, a heart must be really listening, really wanting the truth, really wanting God.*
>
> RUTH BURROWS

MIND AND IMAGINATION

If anyone loves me he will keep my word,
and my Father will love him,
and we shall come to him
and make our home with him.

In the last reflection we began to perceive how it is possible to 'pray the Gospels' as opposed to simply reading them. All it involved was choosing a passage of Scripture, setting aside the time to be still, listening and letting the words speak to us. So far so good, but what will happen at times is – nothing at all. I might be so preoccupied with events in my life that I can't seem to concentrate. At other times I might slip straightaway into deep reflection.

What we need to keep in mind is that, either way, all is well. If our mind is in top gear, rather than trying to switch it off, let it engage the imagination instead. It is often more interesting, anyway, to listen to a radio play than to watch one on television because I can give full rein to my imagination, and that in turn helps to focus my attention better on what is happening, I find.

So it is with the gospel stories. Let us say I have taken the story of the dinner at the house of Simon the Pharisee and the unexpected entrance of the 'undesirable' woman. I might in my imagination become one of the dinner guests, take my place at the table and watch the curious events unfolding with a detached eye, wonder even how I might have reacted. Or I might take the part of the woman herself, imagining how she felt, and translating some of the feelings my imagination has taken from the episode into some event in my own life that this scene has suddenly put me in touch with. A time perhaps when someone pointed the finger at *me*, a painful recollection for a moment. But then as my imagination takes me back to the scene, I am aware of a reassuring tenderness and acceptance, and the accusing Simon is rebuked. The painful memory is eased and I am comforted too.

Of course I am only giving a hypothetical example here. Books on prayer must never attempt to say what *happens* in prayer, because God's work with each individual is utterly individual. But I just want to point out that God works in our imagination too, if we surrender it to him. We must let him be the shepherd of our souls: we might be beside still water, or we might be in the darkened valley – wherever we think or feel we are, he is there working within us. He promises this in the passage above, and we cannot have anywhere closer or more familiar than our home. If we keep our part, making *our* home in his word, that intimate union of God's life and mine – the very purpose of my existence – is guaranteed.

> *I myself will pasture my sheep. I myself will show them where to rest – it is God who speaks. I shall look for the lost one, bring back the stray, bandage the wounded and make the weak strong. I shall watch over the fat and healthy. I shall be a true shepherd to them.*
>
> EZEKIEL 34: 15–16

THE SIMPLICITY OF PRAYER

The simplicity of prayer, its sheer terrifying uncomplicatedness, seems to be the last thing most of us either know or want to know. It is not difficult to intellectualise about prayer – like love, beauty, motherhood, it quickly sets our eloquence aflow. It is not difficult but it is perfectly futile.

SISTER WENDY BECKETT

For me this is one of the wisest counsels on prayer I have come across, in itself a penetratingly simple insight into the journey of prayer which can help travel light years along the way. But there is one curious word in it that seems to jump up out of the page. Why should simplicity be terrifying? I think people find the idea terrifying because when faced with the awesome concept of communicating with God the creator of life they believe it *ought* to be complicated. Heaven knows, it can be almost impossible to get to see the chairman of a large company, but God!

The understandable reaction is to put space between us and God and fill it with comforting ritual, or to systematise prayer by cataloguing it into different degrees of meditation and purification, into prayers of this state or that stage. The strange thing is that there's not a word about any of it in the Gospels, only one simple guideline marked for our special attention: love God, love others and love yourself. But if we have insulated ourselves with all the paraphernalia of prayer, when it is stripped away the exposure *is* terrifying.

Complications do indeed set in when we start to analyse and

[193]

intellectualise. I am reminded of the story of the athlete who, through dedication and training, had acquired a natural effective rhythm in his running that so impressed the experts that they decided to examine this phenomenon. They measured his heart beat, lung capacity, energy conversion rate, muscle extension, balance, bone structure, the lot, and marvelled how all this could come together in one man. So did the athlete when it was all explained to him, and the next time he went out to run he fell flat on his face!

In the journey of prayer we, like the athlete, have to dedicate ourselves to training to begin with – by becoming familiar with the Scriptures and spending time reflecting on the Gospels, and in due course developing a regular rhythm of prayer-time. But once a person becomes fully integrated into the gospel teaching, prayer becomes even more simple: he or she can just literally sit in the presence of God, letting go of self and in faith allowing God to be mystery. As the psalmist described it, like a weaned child on its mother's breast. No anxiety, no activity, in repose and letting my mind go where it will. Certainly no prayer expert making progress reports on how the psychic temperature is faring. All we can do is surrender to God's work, which may be terrifyingly uncomplicated but blessedly so.

> If you desire to stand surrendered before God, then you are standing there. It needs absolutely nothing else. Prayer is the last thing we should feel discouraged about. It concerns nobody except God always longing to give Himself in love – and my own decision. And that too is God's 'who works in us to will and effect'. In a very true sense there is nothing more to say about prayer – 'the simplest thing out'.

SISTER WENDY BECKETT

THE LIGHT OF LIFE

I am the light of the world;
anyone who follows me will not be walking in the dark;
he will have the light of life.

JOHN 8: 12

We touched earlier on the apparent paradox of the spiritual life: the mystery of God's presence which is so often characterised as darkness or (by St John of the Cross) as 'night to the soul', and the whole of revelation in the Scriptures which summons us to the light 'which the darkness cannot overpower' (John 1: 5). There is really no ambiguity here, for in the journey of prayer we are dealing with the two levels of existence which we have referred to from the beginning as the life of the spirit and the life of the flesh: the interior life and the exterior, distinct in themselves yet at the same time inseparable.

They are distinct because when we give the time and space to God his work within us is secret, hidden from our intellect. They are inseparable because the only evidence we will have of God's presence within us will be our changing perceptions and growing understanding in our daily life. The cause is wrapped in darkness and mystery, but the effect is illuminated with the light of life. Faith, like the tiny mustard seed in the darkness of the earth, germinates and is nurtured into growth in secret but it matures and flowers in the light of the sun.

Prayer extends beyond the half hour or hour we give to God: we don't say, well, that's that and switch off till the next session. Prayer enables us to watch for God in all the circumstances of our lives. In the Old Testament the man who

searches for God is described as the watchman who keeps vigil
at the gates of the city, always on the lookout. Like him, if we
wait on God, accept that his work is hidden from any felt
experience, stay faithful to our prayer-time, we will learn how
to listen to his voice – 'the still small voice' – in the life that goes
on around us and perceive his purpose.

Look at life and you're looking directly at God. He lives in art
and nature, people, animals, world events, even soap operas –
everything under the sun. But prayer is where we learn to
recognise him, prayer is where we receive this new dimension
to our day-to-day experience. In prayer it is God who, in the
words of St Paul, puts both the will and action into us
according to his own loving purpose.

> *The kingdom of heaven is like a mustard seed which
> a man took and sowed in his field. It is the smallest
> of all the seeds, but when it has grown it is the
> biggest shrub of all and becomes a tree so that the
> birds of the air come and shelter in its branches.*

MATTHEW 13: 31–2

HAPPY THE EARS THAT HEAR

For the heart of this nation has grown coarse,
their ears are dull of hearing,
and they have shut their eyes,
for fear they should see with their eyes,
hear with their ears,
understand with their heart,
and be converted and be healed by me.
But happy are your eyes because they see,
your ears because they hear!

MATTHEW 13: 15–16

It is a frightening thing, says the unknown author of the Letter to the Hebrews, to fall into the hands of the living God. The same sentiments are still shared by so many people today who will do anything to *avoid* meeting God in prayer. What will it involve, what will it mean? Their hearts are fraught with preconceived ideas of what God is like – not a million miles from those false images of God we observed earlier on. The effects of this can render us fearful and resistant of leaving the security of our carefully constructed protective shells.

Yet over and over again we hear the same words in Scripture: 'Do not be afraid!' God is a gentle father, tender mother, compassionate and full of mercy. Whatever I fear in myself, whatever sins I may have committed or accuse myself of, what awaits me in prayer is profound understanding, forgiveness and healing. 'Come to me all you who labour and are heavily burdened, and I will give you rest.' What needless burdens people carry through deafness to the true source of peace.

[197]

God does not make demands we cannot meet; there is no hint of condemnation in his Spirit that touches us in prayer. Instead we are gently, gently given light to see the truth set before us, and as we grow to understand it so we begin to make the right choices – freely. This is not going to turn me into a saint (or even an angel) – on the contrary it will give me greater insight into what it means to have a fallen nature – but the growth of love in prayer makes me inwardly stronger and less susceptible to the tendencies of evil. Control of self is a gift of the Spirit.

If you really love someone it is impossible consciously or calculatedly to injure them. In the same way the tightening bond of love in relationship with God will make it harder and harder seriously to damage that relationship. This is not out of some heroic pride in putting God first as an act of self-denial. Not at all, it will simply be impossible for someone who has tasted the sweetness of this bonding of love to want to damage or destroy it.

'Your love is better than life' says the psalmist, and there in a nutshell is the whole significance of conversion: coming to the realisation that God's love is better than all life without him has to offer. This we can only know through prayer. We will still be the fallen, fragile creatures we always were, but we will know how to cling to the only source of strength, which is our daily prayer in which God himself holds us fast.

> *For your love is better than life.*
> *My lips will speak your praise.*
> *On my bed I remember you,*
> *On you I muse through the night,*
> *for you have been my help.*
> *In the shadow of your wings I rejoice.*
> *My soul clings to you,*
> *your right hand holds me fast.*

PSALM 62/63: 4, 7–9

CHAPTER ELEVEN

A New Creation

BEHOLD I MAKE ALL
THINGS NEW

For anyone who is in Christ there is a new creation;
the old creation has gone, and now the new one is
here.

2 CORINTHIANS 5: 17

What happens when I present myself to God in prayer is
something I can neither see nor feel, which does make it rather
difficult to describe! But in trying to understand it I find myself
returning time and again to the familiar scriptural images, and
in particular that of the potter fashioning the clay. (I sometimes wonder if that has anything to do with memories of that
hypnotic potter's wheel which was constantly on our screens
in the days when television used to have 'interludes'?)

The spiritual life begins only as a raw material, a formless lump
of clay, which needs to be carefully fashioned to become
something of rarity and beauty, or even of practical value come
to that. The potter works gently, almost imperceptibly; sometimes – as happened when God took Jeremiah down to the
potter's workshop (18: 1) – the clay collapses or goes out of
shape, and then the potter starts afresh. But always the work
goes on until the beauty that was always intrinsic in that lump
of clay becomes visible.

The intrinsic beauty is what is unique to each human being, but
the flaws and ugliness are common to all. When we read that
'the sins of the fathers are visited upon the children through
countless generations' what it refers to is the incompleteness of
people's lives having a roll-on effect on others. A suffers from

[201]

depression because she was not shown any love by her parents, whose capacity for showing love was frozen from yet another cause. B had a mother who dominated his childhood, so that the rest of his life is spent punishing women in order to prove his manliness. C was so affected by her stepfather's cruelty to her mother that she was left with a secret hatred of men and whose daughters, nurtured on this attitude, all had failed marriages. And so it goes on, a sort of emotional domino theory where a person's behaviour is linked to their circumstances, is part of the collective dis-ease of an as yet incomplete human race.

Only 'a new creation' can reshape the pattern, beginning in each of us individually. The life of prayer is one in which the ugly clay yields itself to the potter to reshape and reform its distorted image. We start to yield ourselves to this transformation without understanding the precise nature of our ugliness. It is he who reveals it and with perfect skill removes it.

> *'Get up and make your way down to the potter's house; there I shall let you hear what I have to say.' So I went down to the potter's house; and there he was, working at the wheel. And whenever the vessel he was making came out wrong, as happens with the clay handled by potters, he would start afresh and work it into another vessel, as potters do.*

JEREMIAH 18: 2–5

THE GENTLE GOD

> *'Sir,' said the woman 'give me some of that water, so that I may never get thirsty and never have to come here again to draw water.' 'Go and call your husband' said Jesus to her 'and come back here.' The woman answered, 'I have no husband.' He said to her, 'You are right to say "I have no husband", for although you have had five, the one you have now is not your husband. You spoke the truth there.'*
>
> JOHN 4: 15–19

The work of the Spirit within us is a mystery hidden from us, but in the Gospels we do get glimpses of God at work on human frailty, all of which are inexhaustible sources for reflection – and none more so than the encounter between Jesus and the woman at the well. It took place in a Samaritan town, as Jesus and the disciples were returning to Galilee. It was noon and Jesus was resting by the well when a woman came to draw water: he asks her for a drink of water, and as they talk he explains to her that had she known who he was she could have had the gift of 'living water'.

At first she is perplexed because he 'has no bucket and the well is deep', but it dawns on her that Jesus is not speaking literally and then she wants to know how she can obtain the water that 'will turn into a spring, welling up to eternal life'. Clearly she is a person with those personality defects we examined in the last reflection, clearly she has a longing that her own life's deep thirst should be quenched. Note that she asks for what Jesus offers without understanding it – in just the same way that someone's decision to pray is made without understanding, but is rooted in the *desire* for what God is offering.

How can the truth be revealed to this woman, the truth without which she will remain emotionally crippled? Gently, is the answer, with a gentle subtlety that would be the envy of any modern psychiatrist! Jesus coaxes the woman into facing her problem, not by pointing the accusing finger but by allowing her to see for herself that she has real problems with relationships – and more importantly, to admit it.

You can't answer your own insatiable thirst for love. No amount of new relationships can fulfil your deepest longing, only God and 'God is spirit' Jesus explains to her, 'and those who worship must worship in spirit and truth'. He is saying that we cannot approach God without approaching the truth about ourselves and our lives. Few if any of our problems arise from actual sin but rather from our impoverished circumstances, and this the light of truth can reveal to us.

As we begin to understand ourselves then we can feel understood; as we begin to feel understood, so we can forgive ourselves, and instead of living with our guilt and self-condemnation we can allow God to heal us. That is the cycle of the new creation: seeing, understanding, forgiving, healing, moving forward. The woman drops her water-jar which represents all her personal striving for fulfilment, and runs forward to tell others of her new-found life.

> *Blessed be the God and Father of our Lord Jesus Christ, a gentle Father and the God of all consolation, who comforts us in all our sorrows, so that we can offer others, in their sorrows, the consolation that we have received from God ourselves. Indeed, as the sufferings of Christ overflow to us, so, through Christ, does our consolation overflow.*

2 CORINTHIANS 1: 3–5

THE FULLNESS OF LIFE

I have come
so that they may have life
and have it to the full.

JOHN 10: 10

Earlier we spoke of the incompleteness of human life and the whole of creation being an as yet unfinished symphony. The psalmist catches the imagery beautifully: 'You send forth your spirit and they are created. You renew the face of the earth' (103/104). This life-renewing Spirit of God, that works so intimately with the spirit of an individual, is communicated by Jesus in strikingly simple language. We are asked to imagine a shepherd whose sheep, because they live in such close proximity to him, even know the sound of his voice and learn to follow him because they recognise it.

The people who live, as it were, in close proximity to God are those who make a commitment to prayer, and those who know his voice are those who constantly reflect on the Gospels so that with deep familiarity comes a gradual understanding of the message. The call, say the Scriptures, is by name (as even today in the Middle East the shepherds still know their sheep by individual names) and it will be heard and understood by those who seriously give time to God in prayer.

The call is to self-knowledge, which is a painful process we naturally shrink from. Our instinct is for self-justification – like Eve blaming it all on the serpent, and Adam blaming it all on Eve. To make an observation that has no direct bearing on religion, I would say that what distinguishes greatness from

[205]

mediocrity in a person is an ability to admit freely being wrong about something without putting the blame elsewhere.

The inability to perceive the truth about one's own fallibility is pride, and pride is the first thing prayer must pull down (like the mighty from their thrones). I once heard an American preacher compare the spiritual life with getting into an elevator: contrary to one's natural inclinations you have to learn to push the 'down' button first. The only way up in the spiritual life, he said, was down.

His analogy is valid enough, of course, but if only it were as easy as pushing a lift button! But most of the time we are fearful of self-knowledge, afraid we can't measure up: we need the reassuring symbols and imagery that the Gospels offer us. The good shepherd *does* lead us in our prayer, stays in close proximity, does call us by name. His gentle voice will purify us of our pride, relieve us of the anxious tension of it, and in the end reveal the new life of peaceful self-acceptance. 'I have come so that they may have life and have it to the full.'

> . . . *the sheep hear his voice, one by one he calls his own sheep and leads them out. When he has brought out his flock he goes ahead of them, and the sheep follow because they know his voice. I am the good shepherd; I know my own and my own know me, just as the Father knows me and I know the Father; and I lay down my life for my sheep. And there are other sheep I have that are not of this fold, and these I have to lead as well. They too will listen to my voice, and there will be only one flock, and one shepherd.*
>
> JOHN 10: 3–5, 14–16

PRAYER AND LIFE (1)

You must give up your old way of life; you must put aside your old self, which gets corrupted by following illusory desires. Your mind must be renewed by a spiritual revolution, so that you can put on the new self that has been created in God's way, in the goodness and holiness of the truth.

EPHESIANS 4: 22–4

So how does God begin the work of purification within us, to bring us to the new life we have spoken of? For a start, he does not do it by making crash demands for immediate change; rather it is a process of gradual enlightenment, which first allows us to see our own lives with a new perspective which in turn informs us how to *let* the old creation pass away to be replaced by the new.

I have a reflection on the call to new life which, though a personal one, is shared in some degree by many others, I suspect. Certainly when I share it at a talk or retreat it never fails to find a resonance within the group. In the early stages of my commitment to an hour a day before God, the first thing I became aware of was my perpetual feeling of exhaustion. A prosaic revelation perhaps, but the stillness and silence not only made me more sensitive to it but also helped me to define it as a problem. In that frame of mind I began to think it through, to look for reasons.

For the first time I began to question all the frantic activity in my life and, above all, to examine my motives for much of what was occupying me so industriously. What emerged under

self-scrutiny was an image of myself as a would-be super-
woman trying, if only subconsciously, to save the entire
human race from its problems single-handed. When asked to
do something, no was a word I didn't know how to use. A
classic case of muscular Christianity, submerged in a flurry of
'good works' and 'loving people' by sheer effort – because I
mistakenly thought this was what was required.

Clearly, as I began to see, something was wrong, but only by
delving deeper could I discern that my motives for all this were
far from loving. The real reason for all this angelic vigour was
the resident little snake who lives in the human heart, called
ego. I was actually seeking the approval of others, helping
myself to it and slaving away so as to earn it.

In prayer we are forced back on ourselves and, however
unpalatable, have to learn to confront our poverty. In the
stillness and silence the root cause of my problem was revealed, a problem which is, I believe, a universal one: on the
bottom line we do not love or accept ourselves. We therefore
mistakenly feel we have to make ourselves lovable. We have it
written in our flesh (as Ruth Burrows puts it) that we have to
earn God's love. Without the insight prayer can afford us we
have no real perception of our own unique beauty, nor of his
unconditional love for us no matter how we are.

Through a commitment to prayer I was offered my first
glimpse of new life, a recognition that what I had interpreted as
life-giving was in fact destructive: I was worn out with futile
activity which achieved nothing for myself, for others or for
God.

> *And if the Spirit of him who raised Jesus from the
> dead is living in you, then he who raised Jesus from
> the dead will give life to your own mortal bodies
> through his Spirit living in you.*
> ROMANS 8: 11

PRAYER AND LIFE (2)

It was Peter who answered. 'Lord,' he said 'if it is you, tell me to come to you across the water.' 'Come' said Jesus. Then Peter got out of the boat and started walking towards Jesus across the water, but as soon as he felt the force of the wind, he took fright and began to sink. 'Lord! Save me!' he cried. Jesus put out his hand at once and held him. 'Man of little faith' he said 'why did you doubt?'

MATTHEW 14: 28–31

The experience I described in the last reflection is obviously a very personal one, but by no means untypical as an example of the beginnings of a new creation in the life of an individual. There are parallels, I suppose, with psychoanalysis, in identifying the problems and getting to the source of them. But there is one salient difference: in prayer we are invited to forget the past and fix our eyes on the future.

What I observed in myself was something that prompted a response, a change of direction. In practice it was a venture into unknown territory – learning to say 'no' without feeling guilty, unravelling a carefully woven reputation (how many of us have been nurtured on the specious notion that we must *try* to please all the people all the time at all costs?). Responding to a new offer of life is a veritable walking on water, but it is one that can be undertaken with the sure knowledge that we are not alone. God is right there – closer than we can possibly know – holding us the minute we think we're going to sink.

In my own case there have been storms of protest in my

dealings with people in daily life, but equally there have also been gentle affirmations. The only important test, I have concluded, is what is God asking of me? Without that criterion other occupations are futile. In prayer we are grafted onto a vine which is God's own life, and only this life can produce the appropriate fruit: all the rest has to be pruned, dead actions like dead wood, fit only for the fire. If we are busy with too many things something has to go, and the choices we have to make are what God asks us to, not what will enhance a reputation or avoid conflict. Being a Christian does not mean being a doormat.

In the early stages of my struggle I was given a reassuring witness of God's own saving power in regard to a dear friend who was dying of cancer. She longed, she said one day, to be able to get to a mid-week Mass since Sundays seemed so far apart and time was not on her side. But the Mass was three miles away and she had no transport. What a struggle I had not to leap in there and then with my impulsive angel-of-mercy act and offer to take her – yet I was not free to do so. A week later during a visit she explained how the very day she had told me of her wish, another friend had come to visit and revealed how much *he* would like to go to mid-week Mass, but he could no longer afford the petrol after his recent redundancy. From that moment on they both went each week, he driving, she paying for the petrol! Not only did two other people benefit in this ordinary little incident, I'm sure I did too, from the enlightenment that God can look after his beloved children without my help.

> *Make your home in me as I make mine in you.*
> *As a branch cannot bear fruit all by itself*
> *but must remain part of the vine,*
> *neither can you unless you remain in me.*
> *I am the vine,*
> *you are the branches.*
> *Whoever remains in me, with me in him,*
> *bears fruit in plenty.*
>
> JOHN 15: 4–5

A PEOPLE SET APART

Christ was established as Lord of all by his resurrection – the Lord to whom all authority in heaven and on earth has been given. He still works in the hearts of men by the power of his Holy Spirit, and he does not merely rouse our desire for the world to come; at the same time he stimulates, purifies, reinforces those generous aspirations by which the human family bends its energies to make its own life more humane and to subdue the earth to this purpose.

The Church in the Modern World

In Peter's First Letter he describes the early Church as a consecrated nation, a people set apart, but one has to say that of all the descriptions this one has suffered most from misinterpretation. From the very earliest times the so-called 'chosen' people of God were thus always for the benefit of the entire world. The whole concept of priesthood in the Old Testament was mediatory, and sacrificial offerings strictly on behalf of the whole community.

The distortion arises when the notion of exclusivity creeps in, when people interpret religion as a badge of superior status, a holy huddle who are separate because they are special. Personally I react against all things labelled 'religious' because I cannot conceive of any part of religion that does not belong to the whole human family. If the Church does not exist for the world, then it exists for nothing at all, and that is as true for its individual members as it is for it in a collective sense.

Every true Christian is a part of the on-going incarnation: as St

Paul expressed it 'I live now not with my own life but with the life of Christ' (Galatians 2: 20). And Jesus made it quite clear – 'When I am lifted up from the earth, I shall draw *all* men to myself (John 12: 32). In order to take on the fullness of this life of Christ every Christian has to be a person of prayer, and in their commitment to this have to set themselves apart for a space – but they do so not for their own spiritual gratification, but on behalf of the world. It's a vocation like any other which the community at large benefits from, no different from, say, a ballet dancer who spends long hours perfecting her dance not to perform to an empty auditorium but to give joy to thousands.

They are, to return to the Scriptures yet again, the leaven in the dough, an integral and active part of the whole which by its influence helps the dough to fulfil its purpose. Yes, I do set myself apart to pray every day, but the hope is that the words of Scripture will become embodied in me, that if God is present in me he will be present in all I do, unseen and unfelt but present nonetheless, and that I carry that blessing wherever I go and whether I'm writing about prayer or cooking. ('I'm convinced he shows the same interest in helping people to cook as he does in helping them to pray!') All life is God's life. The Church, or the community of believers, is a vital part of the whole human body, acting continually as purifier, stimulator and reinforcer.

> *The gifts of the Spirit are various. He calls some to bear witness clearly to the desire for heaven and to keep that desire alive among men. Others he calls to devote themselves to serving humanity here – a ministry which provides material for the kingdom of heaven. To all he brings liberation, that setting aside self-interest and putting all earth's powers to human purposes, they may reach out towards a future in which humanity itself will become an offering acceptable to God.*
>
> *The Church in the Modern World*

PLANTED AND BUILT ON LOVE

Out of his infinite glory, may he give you the power through his Spirit for your hidden self to grow strong, so that Christ may live in your hearts through faith, and then, planted in love and built on love, you will with all the saints have strength to grasp the breadth and length, the height and the depth; until, knowing the love of Christ, which is beyond all knowledge, you are filled with the utter fullness of God.

EPHESIANS 3: 16–19

St Paul rather eloquently describes the 'new creation' offered by God to each of us as 'the hidden self growing strong'. That is, the embryonic spiritual life that is in everyone beginning to expand and develop through prayer. This growth is rooted in love as he says, and though we do not know *how* it happens (for 'the Spirit breathes where he wills. Like the wind, you cannot tell where it comes from or where it is going'), yet sometimes imperceptibly, sometimes undeniably, we are coaxed along the path of love. Self is quietly eroded – if we respond and then to the degree we want it to be.

Of course at any point and at any time we can refuse. There will always be sticking-points, those times when we want to evade the issue and cling to self. Then God for his part has to wait patiently till we decide to choose love instead of self. I confess I find the struggle for love an on-going battle: almost all my preconceptions of what loving is seem to have been turned upside down. When the chips are down – as St Peter

[213]

discovered outside the house of Caiaphas when the cock crowed – words and feelings have nothing to do with loving. I have discovered too the shallowness of the love that is simply surrendering to everyone for a quiet life, and equally how costly it can be to stand in truth and challenge someone else's selfishness as an act of love for them. Yet I have come to believe that to be aware of my own impoverished capacity for true love is in itself a most blessed thing, because it continually reminds me (as I fail 'seventy times seven a day') of my absolute need for God.

Paul says 'you must *want* love more than anything' and therein lies one of the paradoxes of prayer: the more it helps us to see the reality, the more we perceive our own poverty in being so far away from it. Love involves the complete sacrifice of self and, if we're honest, we can only concede the impossibility of this. But the answer lies in the words of Jesus: 'For man it is indeed impossible, but nothing is impossible with God.'

These were the words that came to mind recently when I met a beautiful young woman who complained she was in an 'impossible' situation. She had discovered the spiritual side of life, she said, had become more and more contemplative, interested in spiritual reading and having a meaningful relationship with God. But all this was at odds with the demands of her husband's busy career, the social life of entertaining and being entertained in which she was expected to play a full part. She was beginning to find other people 'very materialistic'. I do not know, nor can I predict, the outcome of her story but I do know that a serious commitment to prayer will offer her a new perspective on her problem, that it will enable her to do what may not be humanly possible – that is not only to surrender herself completely but also to discover that in every death there is resurrection and that untold joy awaits us at every moment of surrender. I do know, too, that God can do 'infinitely more than we can ask or imagine' (Ephesians 3: 20) and that in time prayer will reveal her situation as quite different from her imagining when viewed from the deeper perception of truth.

I would end this reflection by referring back to the first chapter (page 20) and the passage from Balthasar on how God's love radiates and instils itself into the hearts of men and women. This is the new creation that is brought forth in prayer.

CHAPTER TWELVE

How Happy are the Poor in Spirit

BY FAITH AND NOT BY SIGHT

> *Among all creatures, the highest and the lowest,
> there is not one that remotely resembles God. Yet
> we naturally persist in confusing Him with crea-
> tures, seeing Him alongside them, as one of them in
> fact, albeit the mightiest and greatest. God trans-
> cends the intellect and is inaccessible to it. How
> far-reaching the consequences of this truth. God
> Himself is 'night to the soul' in this life and man,
> rational finite man, is 'towards' this inaccessible one
> and can find fulfilment only in Him.*

> RUTH BURROWS: *Ascent to Love*

Six hundred years before Christ Isaiah wrote 'Truly you are a
God who lies hidden'. Moses before him, crouched in the cave,
could only catch a glimpse of the back of God, for 'no man can
see God and live'. Jesus' parting words to his disciples were
'You believe me because you have seen me; happy are those
who have not seen yet believe'. St Paul advised that we must
live 'by faith, not by sight'.

Not to see but still to believe is the message of the first
beatitude (which is the title of this chapter). God is beyond
human experience, and whoever comes to terms with this is
one who understands what it means to be merely human and
not God. Being 'poor in spirit' means I am happy to be what I
am and to allow God to be what he is. If he is hidden to me,
right, I am content not to be able to encompass him with my
intellect and senses. I am at the same time freed from the awful

[219]

pressure of striving to be like him, which will always be impossible at any level.

One of the greatest moments of growth in prayer arrives the day I can as it were walk away from my feelings, discount them completely. People fret because they don't 'feel' God is close, or even that God has 'deserted' them. Spiritual writers have compared this anguish to being in a desert, nothing to the front, nothing behind, just me and God – and he totally hidden. Being poor in spirit is being happy with this state, happy as a rational creature to surrender oneself trustingly to this hiddenness.

But, you may be asking, how can we believe we have a relationship with God if we can't feel it? Once again I think what happens in a human relationship can be illuminating. When a new relationship between a man and woman is formed, they don't initially fall in love, whatever the song-writers may say: they fall into feelings. What 'I love you' really means is I love how I feel with you, how you make me feel. The love is self-focused. When the first flush and fervour is over, what is left is a commitment to the other which is a liberation from feelings, a process of shifting the focus from self and learning to love without selfish motives.

Conversion, Morris West once wrote, always begins with falling in love. 'Finding' God we really feel he is so close to us: our faith may even move a few mountains simply because we feel it will. But this is a reflection of our own fashioning. If he disappears from our 'view' of him, as surely happens, it is we who have changed not he. He is as close as ever we *thought* he was, as we have begun the journey of commitment. We now live not by the illusions of sight but – what is far more precious – by pure and simple faith.

> *Where have you hidden yourself, O my beloved?*
> *You leave me in my groanings.*
> *Shy as the deer you have fled away*
> *leaving me wounded.*
> *I ran after you crying, but you were gone!*
>
> ST JOHN OF THE CROSS

THÉRÈSE

Ah! do let us stay very far from all that is brilliant.
Let us love our littleness, love to feel nothing; then
we shall be poor in spirit – and Jesus will come for us
far off as we are. He will transform us . . .

ST THÉRÈSE OF LISIEUX

The theme of this chapter was bound to bring me sooner or
later to a spiritual writer who not only personified the first
beatitude but who is, I am deeply convinced, the supreme
teacher in regard to the spiritual life. The French Carmelite
nun, Thérèse of Lisieux, died at the age of twenty-four, but in
her short life she epitomised the essence of what a relationship
with God involves. She had studied the works of St John of the
Cross, lived his teachings, and was then able to refine them to a
degree of simplicity which, to use a modern idiom, might be
described as a 'short cut' on the whole spiritual journey.

Thérèse is often overlooked today, partly because her language
(that of the late nineteenth-century French bourgeoisie) was
off-putting, partly because of the veneer of sweet-scented piety
that the early twentieth century applied to her. The result is
that the true face of Thérèse has remained very largely hidden.
But she is certainly the writer who has influenced me personally the most (until I discovered Ruth Burrows' work ten years
ago, which for me anyway is pure Thérèse interpreted for the
modern way of thinking). Thérèse's writings do not yield their
treasures instantly – I still have much to learn after twenty-six
years of reading them! The spiritual life can only be lived, and
anything we read is only so much dead wood until we encounter its truth in our own experience, and this happens only to the
degree we want it to.

[221]

But what of Thérèse's 'short cut'? In fact it is no more nor less than what the Gospels themselves offer, which is *simplicity* at every level. Not a shallow lightweight spirituality, such as you can find in a hundred pious devotional books, but a simplicity of enormous depth, one that has been described as a gold mine that offers more and more gold the deeper you dig.

Her message reached the world at the right moment, just as there was an evolution away from centuries of pious practices and 'religious' religion; she helped to establish the spiritual life firmly in the mainstream of human existence where it rightly belongs. Prayer *is* life, and life is prayer. The time given specifically to God, prayer-time, is only the springboard to launch us into the fullest experience of life.

Thérèse understood this and cut through all the peripheral pieties. She called her way of prayer 'the little way' of child-like trust and confidence. But what is said so simply takes a lifetime to grasp in its implications. We can say we understand it, but to really live it . . . ? For the moment let Thérèse have the last word:

I expect nothing of myself but everything of God.

THÉRÈSE OF LISIEUX

LITTLE CHILDREN

*At this time the disciples came to Jesus and said,
'Who is the greatest in the kingdom of heaven?' So
he called a little child to him and set the child in front
of them. Then he said, 'I tell you solemnly, unless
you change and become like little children you will
never enter the kingdom of heaven. And so, the one
who makes himself as little as this little child is the
greatest in the kingdom of heaven.'*

MATTHEW 18: 1–4

It is in the life of Thérèse of Lisieux that this simple teaching of
Jesus is personified. She listened intently not only to the
Gospels but also to the message of her own real guide and
teacher, St John of the Cross, and in doing so caught what is
missed by so many. Jesus didn't just say 'become like children',
he emphasised *little*. To become great is to make yourself as
little as this little child. Little children entrust themselves
utterly to the love and guidance of their parents, unconcerned
about their own standing or status and, even more important,
learning by surrendering to discipline.

Jesus asks his disciples to be spiritually like that – not childish,
but child-like in entrusting responsibility for their spiritual life
to God in the way that a child is totally dependent on its
parents and happy to be that way. Thérèse understood what it
meant to be human with this child-like surrender to a higher
authority. What she referred to as her 'little way' was being
content with the mystery and hiddenness of God. She simply
surrendered herself to God secure in the knowledge that he

alone could transform her hidden spiritual life and weld it to
his own.

She uses an illustration to explain her meaning. God is the sun
(representing love) shining in the heavens, and she is a little
bird who wants to fly and reach the sun by learning to love.
However the bird is too little to get off the ground. It has the
heart and desire of an eagle, this little bird, but it does not have
eagle's wings. All it can do is lift its wings, make the gesture,
and stay on the ground.

Does this cause it sorrow? No, it is content to be little, gazing at
the sun; content even if there are storm clouds hiding the sun.
Sometimes the little bird *feels* as though there is nothing at all
behind the clouds, but this doesn't matter either. It stays there
just the same, not minding that the light is invisible, accepting
in faith that it is there regardless of what it feels or sees.

It keeps up its vigil but, distracted by things of the earth (not
least its own awareness of its feeble weak state of impotence) it
cannot concentrate on this invisible light. But it lives in hope,
even though the radiant love it longs for is out of reach,
confident that eventually it *will* reach the sun of love. The lord
of eagles *will* come himself to take the little, weak bird on his
own strong wings and carry it home himself.

> *In the waste lands he adopts him,*
> *in the howling desert of the wilderness.*
> *He protects him, rears him, guards him*
> *as the pupil of his eye.*
> *Like an eagle watching its nest,*
> *hovering over its young,*
> *he spreads out his wings to hold him,*
> *he supports him on his pinions.*

DEUTERONOMY 32: 10–11

SPIRITUAL PRIDE

Two men went up to the Temple to pray, one a Pharisee, the other a tax-collector. The Pharisee stood there and said this prayer to himself, 'I thank you, God, that I am not grasping, unjust, adulterous like the rest of mankind, and particularly that I am not like this tax-collector here. I fast twice a week; I pay tithes on all I get.' The tax-collector stood some distance away, not daring even to raise his eyes to heaven; but he beat his breast and said, 'God, be merciful to me, a sinner.' This man, I tell you, went home again at rights with God; the other did not. For everyone who exalts himself will be humbled, but the man who humbles himself will be exalted.

LUKE 18: 10–14

It is perhaps easier to grasp what poverty of spirit means by looking at the opposite of it: what is it to refuse to be poor in spirit? Jesus' parable of the two men taking time off to pray illustrates the contrast perfectly. One of them, in Thérèse's terminology, is an eagle, a professional 'spiritual person' set apart from the rest (at least by his own valuation), who does special things for God like fasting and giving alms. He is so proud of his spiritual achievements that he has lost sight of his own limited humanity.

What a contrast to the other man, the little bird. This man is so conscious of his human frailty that he cannot lift his eyes from the ground and can do no more than articulate a plea for mercy. But this is truly prayer untinged by illusions, grounded

[225]

in reality, which in the end is the only path to peace and freedom.

So does it mean I can be grasping, unjust or adulterous so long as I keep praying for mercy? Well, no. What I hope these notes on prayer have shown is that true prayer is an affair of the heart: God hears us in our longing. The tax-collector is paralysed by his struggles but he really does want God, understands his need for him. Pride, on the other hand, is self-sufficient not to say complacent, and that self-sufficiency rules out any *need* for God.

You may recall Jesus' encounter with the rich young man, who suffered a similar problem. Like the Pharisee he had fulfilled all the requirements of the law to the letter, but could not let go of his pride. The advice to him was 'to sell all you have and give it to the poor', which was essentially an exhortation to let go of the source of his self-sufficiency and spiritual achievement, and so allow the truth to flow into his life and through him to others.

The journey of prayer is also a journey into poverty of spirit in the course of which pride is purified away. It is God who does this work, raising up the lowly as well as putting down the mighty. If we're like the woman at the well, poor but not proud, we can respond as she did, bumping into his gentle presence in the ordinary circumstances of our lives. If we're stubborn in our pride, we may well expect to be mowed down in our tracks like Saul on the road to Damascus.

Either way, love is the destination. The translation of the first beatitude I like best is how *happy* are the poor in spirit, for true joy comes of knowing in my heart what it means to be a child of God. 'I thank you, Lord of heaven and earth, for hiding these things from the wise and prudent, and revealing them to mere children' (Luke 10:21).

> *You are mistaken if you believe that your little Thérèse walks always with fervour on the road of virtue. She is weak, very weak, and every day she has*

*a new experience of this weakness, but Jesus is
pleased to teach her, as he did St Paul, the science of
rejoicing in her infirmities (2 Corinthians 12: 5).
This is a great grace and I beg Jesus to teach it to you,
for peace and quiet of heart are to be found there
only. When we see ourselves as so miserable, then
we no longer wish to consider ourselves, and we
look only on the unique Beloved! . . .*

THÉRÈSE OF LISIEUX: *Letter*

LET IT BE DONE UNTO ME

*'The Holy Spirit will come upon you' the angel
answered 'and the power of the Most High will
cover you with its shadow. And so the child will be
holy and will be called Son of God' ... 'I am the
handmaid of the Lord,' said Mary 'let what you
have said be done unto me.'*

LUKE 1: 35, 38

I want to end these reflections on the meaning of poverty of
spirit by going back to the scene of the Annunciation – the very
first moment when the gospel message of salvation was revealed to the ears of the world. At the centre of it is Mary of
Nazareth, not the mythical figure of plaster statuettes and
devotional art, but the human Mary. She sometimes seems
rather a background figure in the Bible, nevertheless she
remains the most enduring character in the four Gospels. She
is present at all the key events: the Annunciation, the birth,
public ministry, death and resurrection of Jesus. Though very
little is said specifically about her, we are given in her life the
very kernel of what the human aspect of being a Christian
means.

I find the most appealing element in her story is that she is
revealed in almost every situation as not understanding what is
happening. 'How can this be?' is the question she asks herself.
It doesn't take much imagination to picture her bewilderment,
which is so utterly akin to our own. Sure, God can do great
things – miracles are ten a penny – but to work a miracle in *my*
very ordinary life! That's something else.

When the angel delivers its message, she does not comprehend

[228]

what it is that God is going to do (or how), but she agrees without understanding. This is faith, pure and simple, consenting to a mystery because in her depths she knows 'nothing is impossible to God'. And this is prayer pure and simple too: I will *let* God do whatever he wants, because at least I understand that is all I can do. I can offer nothing other than myself, and that is the essence of prayer.

In the Gospels Mary has no special status as mother of God. Jesus pointed to his disciples and claimed that *all* were his mother and brother alike: the body of Christ is a community of belief in which no one has a special standing. In fact Mary's life is a model of discipleship: she has to sit at his feet, she ponders all things in her heart, she keeps vigil at the foot of the cross and, finally, she shares in the resurrection.

Likewise we can ponder on God's message of salvation with the same lack of understanding, until it becomes flesh in us too. Like her we wait in shadow with nothing except a sure hope in God's promise. And in our own bitter moments as we stand at the foot of whatever cross we might encounter, we too can do nothing but stand firm in our belief that the promise will be fulfilled. And if like Mary we are faithful, even each moment of dying will be joyful as we move forward to the light of resurrection. If, like her, we say 'let it be done unto me'.

My soul proclaims the greatness of the Lord
and my spirit exults in God my saviour;
because he has looked upon his lowly handmaid.
Yes from this day forward all generations will call me
*   blessed,*
for the Almighty has done great things for me. Holy is
*   his name,*
and his mercy reaches from age to age for those who
*   fear him.*
He has shown the power of his arm,
he has routed the proud of heart.
He has pulled down princes from their thrones and
*   exalted the lowly.*

> *The hungry he has filled with good things, the rich*
> *sent empty away.*
> *He has come to the help of Israel his servant, mindful*
> *of his mercy*
> *– according to the promise he made to our ancestors –*
> *of his mercy to Abraham and to his descendants for*
> *ever.*
>
> LUKE 1: 46–55

INTO THE WILDERNESS

That is why I am going to block her way with thorns,
and wall her in so that she cannot find her way;
she will chase after her lovers and never catch up with
*   them,*
she will search for them and never find them.
Then she will say, 'I will go back to my first husband,
I was happier then than I am today.'
That is why I am going to lure her
and lead her out into the wilderness
and speak to her heart . . .
I am going to give her back her vineyards,
and make the Valley of Achor a gateway of hope.
There she will respond to me as she did when she was
*   young,*
as she did when she came out of the land of Egypt.
When that day comes – it is God who speaks –
she will call me 'My husband'.
When that day comes I will make a treaty on her
*   behalf with the wild animals,*
with the birds of heaven and the creeping things of
*   the earth;*
I will break bow, sword and battle in the country,
and make her sleep secure.
I will betroth you to myself for ever,
betroth you with integrity and justice,
with tenderness and love;
I will betroth you to myself with faithfulness,
and you will come to know the Lord your God.

HOSEA 2: 8–18, 20–2

[231]

Concluding these reflections I want to sum up this journey into God, which we call prayer, by pondering this passage from the prophet Hosea. From the first breath we take our lives are for nothing other than God himself, but it can take the whole of our lives to comprehend this purpose. Yet the whole of this time God is, as it were, hovering, waiting, coaxing us to himself. Here Hosea gives us an allegory of this, in which God is represented as a besotted husband and we as his wandering unfaithful bride.

The bride is blocked by thorns, in the same way as we find ourselves hemmed in by our dissatisfactions and restless longing that cannot be fulfilled by anything the world offers; the thorns symbolise the bitterness that so often forces us to look outside for answers; the lovers that we can never catch up with are the idols we erect, the dreams of our own plans for fulfilment which, when they fade, leave us with the pain of emptiness.

In prayer we are 'lured' into a wilderness where we have no foothold of our own, no self-created security, but where we stand totally exposed to God. Here he speaks to us, not audibly but at heart level, gently drawing us away from our false idols nearer and nearer to himself. I was once privileged to hear this passage expounded by a Hebrew scholar, who pointed out further symbolism. 'I am going to give her back her vineyards' is the whole work of God in restoring us to wholeness and fruitfulness. What is stripped away as we are hemmed in by thorns is all our self-seeking and egotistic motives. The Valley of Achor in Hebrew represents not just suffering but the bitterest thing in a person's life – in God's plan this will become a gateway of hope.

In a way a person has to have experienced this to understand it fully, but Mother Julian understood it as '*all* being well' – that no one entering the full light of revelation at the end of their lives would look back and choose to have had anything altered in any way; even the pain and bitterness can be used in some way and transformed by God for our ultimate good.

She will call me 'My Husband' – this is the moment of truth and complete understanding of who God is, the moment of surrender and final union with God which is the purpose of our life. After that comes the promise of peace, when everything is tamed: the wild beasts of temptation, all our evil inclinations, our egocentricity. God himself will have fought and won the battle. We will be wedded to him for ever in tenderness and love. His faithfulness will last for ever and we will at last have come to know who he is.

> *God, as we have seen, has already transfigured our sufferings by making them serve our conscious fulfilment. In his hands the forces of diminishment have perceptibly become the tool that cuts, carves and polishes within us the stone which is destined to occupy a definite place in the heavenly Jerusalem. But he will do still more, for, as a result of his omnipotence impinging upon our faith, events which show themselves experimentally in our lives as pure loss will become an immediate factor in the union we dream of establishing with him.*
>
> *Uniting oneself means, in every case, migrating, and dying partially in what one loves. But if, as we are sure, this being reduced to nothing in the other must be all the more complete the more we give our attachment to one who is greater than ourselves, then we can set no limits to the tearing up of roots that is involved on our journey into God.*

TEILHARD DE CHARDIN: *Le Milieu Divin*

GUIDELINES FOR PRAYER

The following represent a brief summary of the points we have discussed in the second half of this book. They are essentially practical, a checklist if you like for anyone who wants to embark on the journey of prayer.

* Ask myself, do I want to know God, do I want to try to find the true meaning and purpose of my existence? If the answer is, yes I do, this is going to involve time off the treadmill.

* Time can only be created if I really have made a conscious decision; procrastination only prevails in a situation where no genuine decision has yet been made.

* Once the decision has been made, we must work hard at a commitment to set aside a specific time daily – not absolutely rigid because life never allows for that, but our efforts must be focused on making it a *habit* that becomes a natural part of normal life.

* If you find it difficult to keep still and silent, by all means begin with fifteen minutes daily, but the aim should be to increase this to thirty minutes and ultimately to an hour. This is, after all, *the* most important relationship you will ever have.

* It is most helpful to set aside a place for prayer, a certain corner of a certain room where there will be no phones ringing or people coming and going during the time you have set aside. But do have a clock or watch to hand, so that you do not spend your time trying to guess when fifteen or thirty minutes are up.

* It is important, in the beginning, to reflect on the Scriptures

during prayer-time, especially the Psalms and the Gospels, but a *little* at a time: galloping through whole chapters is pointless. We are learning to receive rather than trying to achieve and this is best done by concentrating on one single Gospel a verse or two at a time. You could for instance begin with Mark, the shortest Gospel, remembering to receive whatever it yields and to leave whatever it does not. As you grow in faith and become more reflective the Gospels will reveal more and more, but in the beginning it's important not to be discouraged by enigmatic passages. Just leave them and move on to something that does touch you or have meaning for you. It is often helpful outside of prayer-time to use a gospel commentary. There are some very helpful and inexpensive commentaries published by Penguin.

Another way to reflect on the Gospels during prayer is to follow the Daily Missal or Alternative Service Book. Either way, what is paramount is to let God reveal himself in whatever way he wishes. It may be that a verse from the Scriptures speaks to us about ourselves, so that we are reflecting less on the Scripture than on something it has triggered off. This is perfectly normal – remember it is God guiding us in our prayer and we have to learn to surrender to whatever he does. St Thérèse sometimes fell asleep during the allotted prayer-time, and what's more was content in what she felt was her human weakness – entirely in keeping with poverty of spirit. Being there totally for God is enough.

* We need never worry about distractions. In one sense distractions can keep us humble, for those whose efforts are concentrated on achieving an empty mind are really focusing on self. We must be prepared to go to God with 'empty hands, to be poor with nothing to give'. All of which is not a licence to 'use' the time for, say, thinking through some project and calling it prayer. Our intentions are what count and they are not hidden from God. If our deepest desire is for him and we let go of ourselves, even if our minds are wandering hither and thither, he will be the Lord of our prayer.

* Emotions and feelings are not important. Some days we may feel close to God, on others that he is remote. But 'for

richer or poorer' we must learn to stick with our commitment, accepting with St Paul 'the loss of everything. I look on everything as so much rubbish if only I can have Christ' (Philippians 3: 8).

* Prayer is life. 'Anyone who follows me will have the light of life as his guide' (John 8: 12) is something that can only be lived, never explained. Whoever is committed to prayer knows that the way to God is through everyday life. It is prayer that opens our spiritual eyes and ears to see and hear him more clearly in all that we do.

* Love is his only meaning, and prayer can never be prayer unless it leads to love.

EPILOGUE

Eros by Paul Klee

The painting which has been reproduced on the cover of this book has a beautiful commentary written by Sister Wendy Beckett, which I have included here as I feel it might be helpful to use in conjunction with the cover for reflection.

To many people, to many artists, 'eros' would mean only physical 'love'. Klee knows that its true meaning is spiritual. In the heart of man there is an aching sense of incompleteness, a need for the Other, the One whose presence and whose love will make us fully human, fully real. Essentially, this Other is God, and only in Him are man and woman each whole and lovely.

But we may not 'experience' God, our holy Lover. So Klee shows the act of prayer as dominated by the human side. The large dominant arrow shoots up from the earth, and the tender ardent arrow of fire that touches its blackness is only seen by the eye of faith.

The great triangle that rises from the earth, emphasising and containing the sharp black arrows of desire – our prayer – is made up of many colours and layers, both vertical and horizontal. Prayer is not an isolated act, Klee says. It is held in being by all we do and are. Every part of our day contains the potential for this act of prayer, yet prayer must have its time set apart because, though sustained by our daily life, it yet is a concentration that is both apart from it and held within it. *All* echoes and re-echoes the central act of prayer. *Nothing* is alien or in opposition and so Klee shows colour of every kind in his arrow.

Of God's triangle and arrow we see little. He is so hidden, so secret, so unattainable by the world, His coloration, as it were, is not ours. But – as Klee shows – if we could see the two together, as we shall in heaven, we would also see that we are made for Him. There is no 'picture' if the gentle secret touch does not come down from above, seeking out and drawing into itself the rough thrusting arrow from below. The one point of fire in the picture is the glow of this almost imperceptible touching, this still and silent union. This is eros in its essence. God's presence in Jesus, taking mankind's helpless longing to Himself. Klee shows us the arrow of man's darkness twice, at the base of the picture, which may in its distracted clumsiness be all we sense, but then again, much smaller and more slender, perhaps beyond our sensing, when the real meeting takes place. The Holy One initiates and draws to Himself all that we are. Prayer is His affair, not ours. Our 'Eros' is His love, His Spirit, His Jesus.